Pocket guide

Balanced Scorecard

The European Approach

Dr. Herwig R. Friedag
Dr. Walter Schmidt

1st English Edition

Translated by Deogratias Emuron, Entebbe, Uganda

Contents

Preface

In this pocket guide we will tell you the story of the Gutleb-Association, a non-profit organisation. This organisation is not only faced with the task of staying afloat in the daily competitive business environment, but it must also, above all, take care for its future: How will this future look like? What can be done better? And how can everyone in a large organisation work towards common goals? In the Balanced Scorecard, Gutleb has found the management tool it needs to achieve this.

What lies behind the Balanced Scorecard? Is it merely a performance management system? What does it have to do with concepts like strategy, key image, vision or mission? We are going to show you the significant potential of this method: With this method, actions of many individuals can be effectively directed towards a common goal!

In a step-by-step process you will be able to understand what a Balanced Scorecard is, its advantages, and how it is developed and implemented – be it in a business or in any other organisation.

We hope that after reading this you have gained a deep insight and understanding: You too can create huge potential and build a brighter future for your company with the Balanced Scorecard!

In the end a big THANKS to Deogratias Emuron, Entebbe, Uganda for high quality translation and to Nicoleta Thomka, Munich, Lucy Bloch-Wehba and Scott Friedag Seaward, New York City for proofreading.

Dr. Herwig R. Friedag, Dr. Walter Schmidt; Berlin - Germany

1   Balanced Scorecard – an Introduction

The long-serving manager of the Gutleb-Association is soon retiring. It is quite understandable that she wishes her "baby" – a large charitable organisation - with a bright future!

And so she lands upon the Balanced Scorecard. What this management tool does, the advantages it brings with it, and the preconditions favouring its success are what you are going to read about in this chapter.

1.1   Do you know Gutleb? Highlights of the association

Hello, I am Brigitte Heumann, Managing Director of the Gutleb-Association in Karlsruhe, Germany. We are a charitable organisation committed to Christian values with 1,200 registered members. As an organisation promoting free social welfare, we consider it our responsibility on the one hand to offer children in nursery schools and day care centres something more than just a "child-care centre" and on the other hand to provide accommodation together with caretakers for senior citizens at reasonable prices.

Our basic position

We are not a special institution. There are hundreds, perhaps even thousands of similar organisations in Germany. Nevertheless, only a few of them have a size comparable to ours:

- More than 6,000 children are looked after daily by 420 members of staff.
- About 2,500 senior citizens are spending the last years of their lives in 83 old people's homes. 900 employees take care of these old people, some of whom even need nursing care, on a part- or full-time basis.
- In addition to the 1,320 "operational" employees, the organisation employs yet another 42 employees in its central administration.

As a charitable organisation we are not supposed to make any profits. Our income is prescribed by the state or the health insurance and insurance institutions to the tune of more than 90% - that leaves us with very little room for manoeuvre. Nevertheless I have hitherto always managed to draw up balanced annual results and for the most part to credit the permitted reserves with a small reserve amount.

However, the two departments contribute differently to the overall results. While the old people's homes generate surpluses every year, the child and youth care services department is generally in a slight deficit.

The following annual results were realized by the Gutleb-Association for the year 2015:

results 2015		Children	Senior citizens	Admin.	Total
Places		6,000	2,500		
Utilised capacity	%	95	97		
Employees	#	420	900	42	1,362
Investments	k€/a	360	2		2
Salaries/Nat.Insur.	k€/a	11	20	2	32
Material expenses	k€/a	5	42	3	50
∑ Expenditure	k€/a	16	62	5	82
Revenue	k€/a	16	68		83
Cash Flow*	k€/a	0	6	-5	1

* Cash Flow = payment surplus or deficits

What is the way forward?

However, this imbalance is not our real problem. There have been a number of rapid changes in the area of non-statutory welfare over the last few years. The old structures are breaking up. Something similar to competition is in the air; be it from private organisations, the workers' welfare association, the joint welfare association or the traditional church institutions like Caritas (catholic church) and Diakonie (protestant church). We must ensure that we do not fall on hard times. Welfare institutions are no longer immune from insolvency too!

Moreover: As I am nearing 60, retirement is rapidly approaching.

And this is how I thought about it:

- Where do we want to go?
- What do we want to achieve?
- Which strengths can we build on?
- Where do we need to do more catching up?
- Where are we faced with threats?

In short - we needed a strategy! And I was fully aware that this would not be done either with "mobilisation slogans" or a "comprehensive package of measures". I wanted more than this. I wanted to achieve sustainable change in organisational culture, because I am convinced that we shall have competitive advantage based on this rationale!

I therefore decided, after consultation with my fellow colleagues in management, to try the Balanced Scorecard. It was Klaus Marwitz, honorary member of the Executive Board of Gutleb-Association and Chairman of the Advisory Board of Marwitz Co. Ltd. & Plc., who introduced the Balanced Scorecard to me.

Lessons from best practice: A couple of years ago Klaus Marwitz was faced with the task of developing a new strategy for his company - a medium-sized manufacturer of gas chromatographs. Three years before that he had lost his younger brother, Thomas, and as sole managing director he had to suddenly assume the command at the age of 70. This had not turned out well until an experienced sales man finally expressed readiness to step in as managing director. The "newcomer" vigorously set about making the company sustainable again. The Balanced Scorecard was a great help to him in that process – and the company is once again standing on solid foundation today.

Why am I telling you all this? It is because I have come to know and appreciate the Balanced Scorecard as a tool which helped us too to find the way forward. Who knows, maybe it could become helpful to you as well!

1.2   What is a Balanced Scorecard?

Definition: The Balanced Scorecard is a universal management tool designed to align actions of a group of people (e. g. organisations, companies, business sectors, project groups) to a common goal.

Originally the Balanced Scorecard came into existence at the beginning of the 1990s as a tool for translating strategies into practice.
Two Americans - Robert S. Kaplan and David P. Norton - had developed an idea in 1992. Their motto was: "Translate strategy into action". And their approach was rather simple: If strategies are to become practical, people must a) understand them and b) be able to translate them into concrete actions.

- It does not suffice to focus one's attention primarily on financial performance ratios like turnover, profit and capital utilization. Those ratios only tell us whether we were successful in the past. They do not tell us anything about the strategic preparations for our future successes through the development of an acceptable idea (vision), the building of close customer relationships, the target-oriented approach of committed employees through learning and growth, the effective consolidation of internal business processes with the help of responsible "process owners" or by guaranteeing a stable financial situation through good relationships with investors.
- And we must be able to distinguish between what is important and what is not, by concentrating on a few important ratios. Why don´t we take a cue from the world of sports? All the essential data is displayed on one single display screen (in the stadium) or on one scorecard (e.g. in golf). In that way we can see at a glance where we are, which tasks have already been completed and what remains to be done.

That is how the idea of the score card was born. And since we cannot translate our strategy into action by ourselves alone, but rather also need the commitment and actions of other relevant interest groups (i.e. stakeholders like customers, fellow workers, suppliers, process owners, investors) in order for us to succeed, the views of these stakeholders regarding our company (referred to as "perspectives" by Kaplan and Norton) should be indicated on the scorecard in a balanced manner, as a true Balanced Scorecard.

Balanced Scorecard according to Kaplan/Norton

Example:

The Gutleb-Association had until now merely focused its whole attention on being profitable and being able to cover its costs. But profitability does not come alone. So for instance, the investment in central kitchen systems had an overall cost-reducing effect on the company in general, but customer satisfaction deteriorated in equal measure, and so the workload for employees increased. The quality of care went down. The hitherto excellent image of the Gutleb-Association became endangered, and with it the targeted growth. That did not please the executive board.

The Balanced Scorecard in practical use

Common features ...

There has been a great variety of Balanced Scorecard manifestations in practical use over the years. Despite all the differences between them, they have the following aspects in common:

1   Formulation of the central strategic key objective (key idea) derived from the "vision".

2   Concretisation of the key objective through sub-goals which are derived from

- Strategic orientation ("strategic topics" or "key success factors") and

- Expectations/goals of the relevant stakeholders with regard to the benefits which our company can bring for them ("perspectives" or "development areas"   for common potentials):

   - Customers,
   - Process owners (internal processes),
   - Fellow workers (learning/development, innovation),
   - Investors (Finance and Controlling),
   - Partners/competitors (suppliers, cooperation partners, corporate group, municipalities etc.).

3   Specification of ratios as measures of the key objective and the selected sub-goals.

4   Derivation of actions which fulfil the sub-goals.

5   Specification of ratios for those actions.

6   Organisation of the common tasks for the practical translation of the strategy into action (projects, programs for action).

7   Integration of the ratios into the controlling-process (Managing with measurable goals).

... and differences

Differences in the practical application of the Balanced Scorecard can essentially be determined on three criteria:

1   In what way is the Balanced Scorecard connected to the strategy of the company?

It is not uncommon for the term "Balanced Scorecard" to be equated with a performance management system. When it comes to practical application, this often leads to a mere compilation of different ratios – most especially in connection with software solutions. That contradicts the original idea put forward by Kaplan and Norton: "Balanced scorecards should not just be collections of financial and non-financial measures - embedded in three to four perspectives. The best Balanced Scorecards reflect the strategy of an organisation." (Kaplan/Norton: The Strategy-Focussed Organization).

However only he who has a strategy can reflect that strategy using ratios! Moreover objectives are, unfortunately, much too often formulated without considering whether they suit each other, and without considering who will translate them into action, when, and with what amount of time and money. It is also questionable whether the people who are supposed to implement those objectives understand and believe in their practical relevance!

> Mark Twain is quoted as having long ago said:
>   "Whoever does not know where he wants to go to should
>   not get surprised if he arrives somewhere else!"

A Balanced scorecard which does not build on a given business idea (identity, vision, mission, core benefit) and on an underlying business model will show little orientating effect. We can only avoid that by formulating a strategy in the run-up to or in the course of designing a Balanced Scorecard. The concrete image we get of our strategy in this way speaks for the need to have a connection with the Balanced Scorecard. We shall turn our attention to this question in the next chapter.

2 How will the people be involved in strategy development and implementation process?

"Translate strategy into action" - that is the task of the Balanced Scorecard: the practical translation of the strategy into daily actions. It is obvious that this task depends on the way the people concerned are integrated into the process. And it is on this very point that the practical cases of application differ considerably.

The scope ranges from strict setting of strategic policy guidelines by the "boss" or by a small selection of management executives to open dialog about individual and common objectives and their translation into a strategy supported by all those involved.

At one end, the Balanced Scorecard is integrated into a setting characterised by hierarchical features and has the tendency of being reduced to a planning and monitoring system. The objectives are "set" and explained in the best way possible. The Balanced Scorecard is used exclusively for the purpose of determining suitable measures for the implementation of the guidelines and having them executed by the employees.

At the other extreme, the Balanced Scorecard forms the framework for the organisation of open structures around a common objective. All management executives and employees are inspired to participate in the development and implementation of the strategy. There is a tendency for this process to remain open because the objectives are always "undergoing testing" and all those involved are ready to learn from their mistakes. In this dynamic environment, the Balanced Scorecard becomes a "learning system" for management and for the development of a "learning company".

3 In which way does the integration of the Balanced Scorecard into the whole structure of corporate action and reporting take place?

The Balanced Scorecard as a strategic performance management system is often assigned to reporting. It therefore could widen the spectrum of already existing reporting systems, but this is not the central task.

On the contrary, Kaplan/ Norton draw attention to the fact that according to their experience, it is indeed those companies and institutions that have developed a new management system using the Balanced Scorecard that exhibit the greatest success - a management system which enables them to create a strategy-focused organisation (Kaplan/Norton, The strategy focused organization). The more we understand the Balanced Scorecard as the" translation of strategies into action by leading with measurable goals", the sooner it will help us to successfully plan the practical daily activities of our customers, workers and partners.

In this connection there are some highly regarded "solutions" of "calculating" the future using the Balanced Scorecard. For that purpose, mathematical interrelationships are developed between the ratios of actions, the so-called "critical" success factors, and the key objective. This can lead to dangerous illusions, because we

- Are quick to overlook the fact that each calculation is based on assumptions whose plausibility and consistency are not normally checked;
- Normally base ourselves on linear correlations when dealing with mathematical models hence fail to sufficiently capture either the inner complexity of an organisation or the delays relating to time and space;
- Pretend apparent accuracy and objectivity when it comes to computer calculations which are often already lacking in source data.

However, there is a tendency for us to hide our subjective responsibility behind objective calculations. The result is that we are faced with soft spots whose consequences are often disastrous. Therefore, we should not surrender to this self-deception.

1.2   The Approach put forward by Kaplan and Norton

Kaplan/Norton developed their Balanced Scorecard within the context of a hierarchical system. The organisational mission, core values, vision and strategy form the basis of their actions. The strategy describes the game plan of the organisation and the Balanced Scorecard spells out its implementation. The people's objectives are, in relation to their function subordinate to the objectives of the organisation.

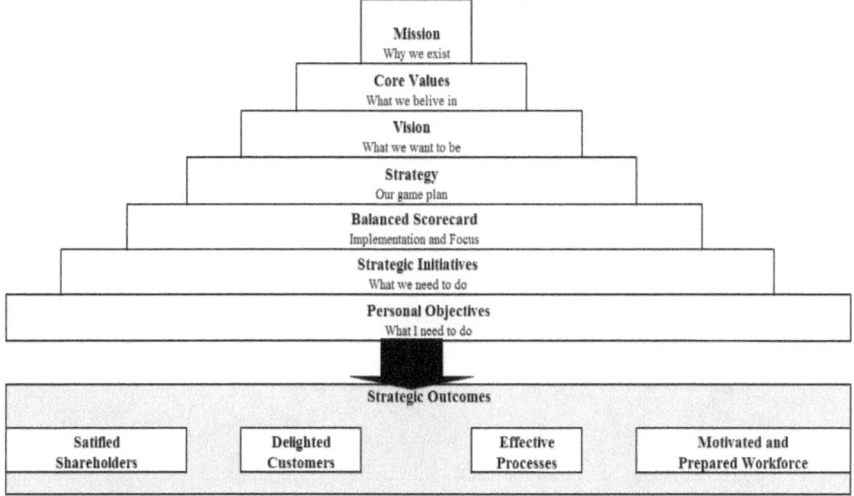

The "pyramid" designed by Kaplan/Norton: Translation of the strategy into desired results
in: The Strategy-Focussed Organization p.73.

In all this the investors (shareholders) are the main focus of attention. The utilisation of their capital is the top-most objective, and the financial perspective is consequently the highest level of a hierarchically structured Balanced Scorecard.

Next in line is the customer perspective which is meant to describe the value proposition that is being made available to the market.

The value chain of the organisation is highlighted in the underlying internal perspective of cooperative interaction. The value chain is comprised of all activities which are necessary for the creation of the offer for the customers and its transformation into growth and profitability.

Finally, the perspective on learning and development as a foundation: this defines the immaterial values required for the elevation of corporate activities and customer relationships to a higher level.

Nevertheless, Kaplan and Norton lay a lot of emphasis on the fact that each company should develop its own Balanced Scorecard and that these four perspectives don't necessarily have to be the ones always being considered. What matters are the views of the stakeholders concerned and these have to be specifically defined in **each** individual case.

Progression of a Balanced Scorecard according to Kaplan/Norton

As a first step, the formulated strategy is illustrated using a "strategy-map". In that process, the objectives of the organisation are placed in a "table" composed of strategic topics and perspectives. The various objectives are subsequently joined together using so- called "cause-and-effect-chains".

Strategy map according to Kaplan/Norton

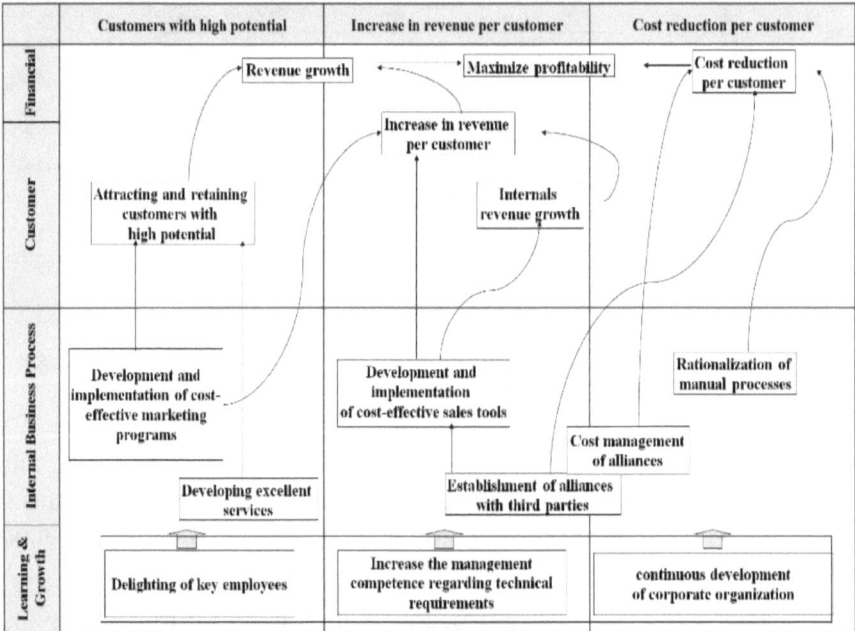

in: The Strategy-Focused Organization

The cause-and-effect-chains are supposed to show the communication channels of the strategy across the entire company. However they convey the simplistic illusions of linear interrelationships and make it hard to comprehend the remote effects of our actions. Admittedly this makes the illustration easy to understand at first sight, but is rather counter-productive for strategic thinking.

- In the second step, objectives from the "strategy map" are transformed into perspectives of the Balanced Scorecard. In the process, the cause-and-effect-chain and the assignment to the strategic topics are not pursued any further. A ratio is set for each objective along with guidelines for the development of that ratio and its relevant measures.
- In the third step derivation of projects or action programs takes place. The projects are in that process mostly tied to the functional structures of the companies:

	Objectives	Measures	Targets	Initiatives		
Financial	Revenue growth				Project ...	
	Maximize profitability				responsible:	
	Cost				Duration of project:	
	...				Ressources:	
Customer	Sales				expected	
	Cross-Selling				utility:	
	Migration				Objective:	
	...					
Internal Business Process	Reliability				Project ...	
	Alliances				responsible:	
	Marketing				Duration of project:	
	...				Ressources:	
Learning & Growth	Key-employees				expected	
	Succession				utility:	
	Culture				Objective:	
	...					

Integration of projects into the Balanced Scorecard according to Kaplan/Norton

This finance-orientated structure does not work for non-profit organisations. That's why Kaplan/Norton have placed mission at the very top of the hierarchy of the Balanced Scorecard (Kaplan/Norton: The Strategy-Focused Organization, p.121). Otherwise the methodology is identical.

The placement of personal objectives at a lower rank below the objectives of the organisation is maintained.

The building of a strategy-focused organisation

Kaplan/Norton did not develop the Balanced Scorecard in isolation. As a management system, it is embedded in the framework of a comprehensive concept of the "Strategy-Focused Organization".

The Principles of a Strategy-Focused Organization

5. Mobilize Change
through Executive Leadership
Mobilization
Governance Process
Strategic Management System

1. Translate
Strategy to
Operational Terms
Strategy Maps
Balanced Scorecards

Balanced Scorecard
Strategy

4. Make Strategy a
Continual Process
Link
Budgets and Strategy
Analytics and
Information Systems
Strategic Learning

2. Align the
Organisation to
the Strategy
Corporate Role
Business Unit Synergies
Shared Service Synergies

3. Make Strategy
Everyone's
Everyday Job
Strategic Awareness
Personal Scorecards
Balanced Paychecks

The Strategy-Focused Organization according to Kaplan/Norton [1]

---

[1] You will find references to publications by Kaplan and Norton in the Literature Index at the end of this pocket guide.

1.3 The European Approach of Friedag and Schmidt

A further development of this method of resolution is practiced by Friedag/Schmidt. In their approach it is the people with their objectives and potentials (possibilities and capabilities) who are the main focus. Several "balances" which are to be drawn up emerge from that, and they are connected with the development and implementation of a Balanced Scorecard:

- The potentials must match the changes which are being strived for together with the objectives.
- Changes often give rise to fears. One knows what one has and is not sure of what one will get. Therefore, changes are easier to realise if the people concerned can associate them with the preservation of their most treasured values and if their identity as a people is not put into question.
- Common values give a meaning to our objectives. But if we need other people to be in "the same boat" with us for the sake of realising our objectives, then our objectives must make sense to those other people too. We have to balance our interests (perspectives) with their interests.
- The different perspectives of those involved must be geared towards the jointly developed objectives for the whole duration of the change. During that process, a set of 4 to 5 ratios can be of help, if they are "coherent" to all participants, i.e.
  - ➤ To make it evident **in a way understandable to them** whether we are on the right track to achieve our objectives and what distance remains to be covered;
  - ➤ They **can be influenced** by the direct players and
  - ➤ They attain practical **meaning** in the daily lives of the people.

Therefore, it is all about meaningful "management with measurable goals" and coherent ratios. It is about bringing together the different perspectives resulting from the various interests of the people.

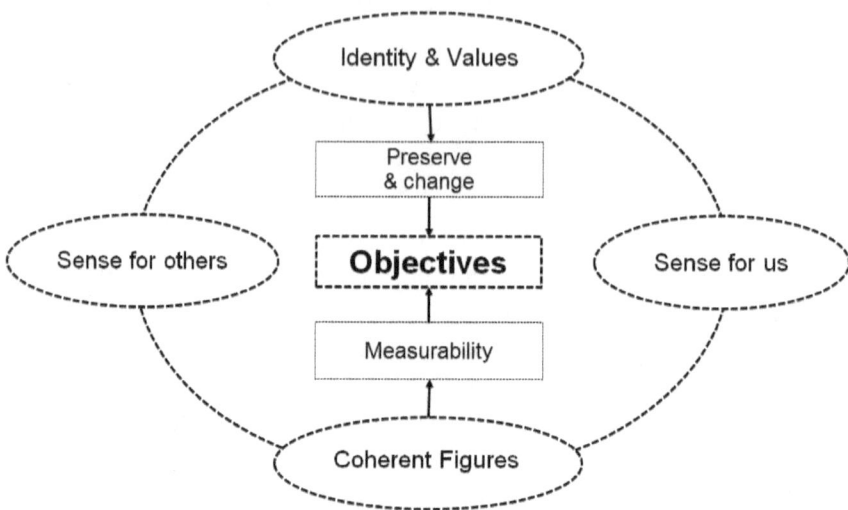

Approach of Friedag/Schmidt: Management with measurable objectives

Finding common objectives

The search for strategy begins with questions like:

- What do we want to preserve? What do we want to change?
- To what extent do we identify ourselves with the company? (Is it part of our own development or just a means to an end? Can we be proud to work here?)
- Which values do we want to have in life (as a group); in order to preserve this or to develop this identity further?
- Who formulates the company's objectives and how are "the others" integrated into the search for those objectives?

The guaranteeing of financial stability seems in this context to be more of an existential principle than an objective. One has to be able to finance one's strategy if it is to be realised. And if that necessitates bringing in investors then they have a right to expect an appropriate return on their invested capital. The objective of the strategies, however, consists in having

a balance between growth, development and profit,

which gives the people room for their personal actualisation.

To that extent the balanced score card does not require hierarchical structures, according to Friedag/Schmidt, to which the objectives of the people involved have to be subjected. The reverse is true; people structure the Balanced Scorecard according to the individual peculiarities of their own objectives and translate them into practical ACTIONS through cooperative interaction.

And there is even no methodical difference between the Balanced Scorecard of a profit making organisation and that of a non-profit organisation.

Progression of a Balanced Scorecard - the European Approach

Friedag and Schmidt begin their approach rightly with a discussion of personal objectives and values. After embedding it there, a jointly-owned strategy is (1) conceived, (2) developed, (3) implemented and (4) used in everyday life:

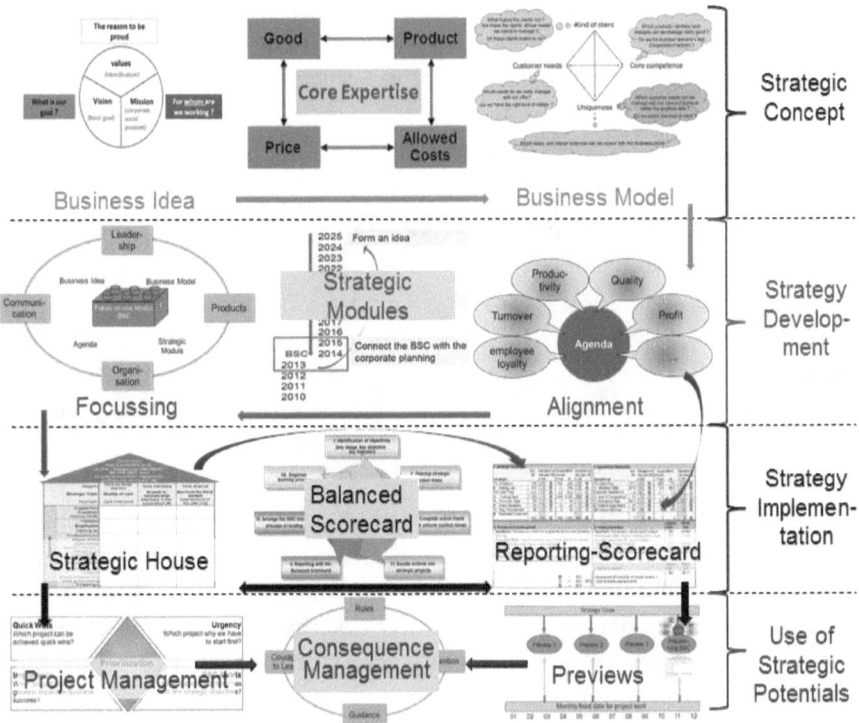

Process -flow for the conception, development, implementation and use of a strategy

1 The strategy concept consists of the combination of a
  - **Business idea** (why we are proud to work here [our values]; what we strive for [vision] and whom we are there for [mission],
  - Strategically effective product or service offer (**core expertise**)
  - Leading **business model** (how we want to earn enough money in order to finance the strategy)
    - What is our uniqueness which is important for the customers?
    - What can we do particularly well and do these core competences give birth to our uniqueness?
    - What do the core needs of our customers consist of, and do our core competencies fit them?
    - Who are our customers? How do these people "tick" with such core needs and do we fit in with each other?
    - Which sales and margin potential is associated with our uniqueness?

2 The strategy development consists of the combination of
  - **Corporate policy orientation** (CPO = Agenda for the central objectives in 5-10 years),
  - **Strategic components** (structuring of the most important decisions for the realization of the agenda) and of
  - **Focusing** on the most important content - related tasks (topic store for leadership, products, organisation and communication).

3 Strategy implementation is centered round the Balanced Scorecard, in a narrow sense of the word (details will be given in the next chapter). In order to be able to take into consideration the different intentions of the people involved, the Balanced Scorecard is developed and designed in 2 coherent but at the same time independently maneuverable parts, according to Friedag/Schmidt:
  - A **Management Balanced Scorecard** which serves the organisation of people's concrete actions when implementing their strategies. We shall dress them in the form of a "strategic house" and
  - A **Reporting Scorecard** which serves responsible management by means of measurable goals and connects strategic management with operational management.

4 Strategy use is centered around "consequence management" in conjunction with

- An effective accompaniment of the projects arising in connection with the strategic house and
- Regular previews for purposes of making a prognosis for attainment of the objectives and the derivation of appropriate measures as well as - if need be - the clarification of the strategy.

A Balanced Scorecard must be simple and understandable for the people who are supposed to implement it. But that is not enough. If the scorecard is to exist in everyday life, it needs the consequence of having to adhere to decisions made.

This European approach by Friedag/Schmidt is base on the example highlighted in this pocket guide (Gutleb-Association).

Further aspects of strategy development are described in the book "Balanced Scorecard - simply consequence " by Friedag/Schmidt, which was published (in German) in 2014.

1.4 Seven Principles

During the development and implementation of a Balanced Scorecard seven principles should be considered:

1 Consistent orientation towards strategic questions

When strategies are translated into practical actions with the help of a Balanced Scorecard it is useful to first understand the difference between operational and strategic action.

We usually equate operative action with something short- termed and strategic action with something long-termed. That is a fallacy. Operational and strategic are not questions of maturity; they relate to the differences in ways of dealing with success potentials
(according to a concept by A. Gälweiler):

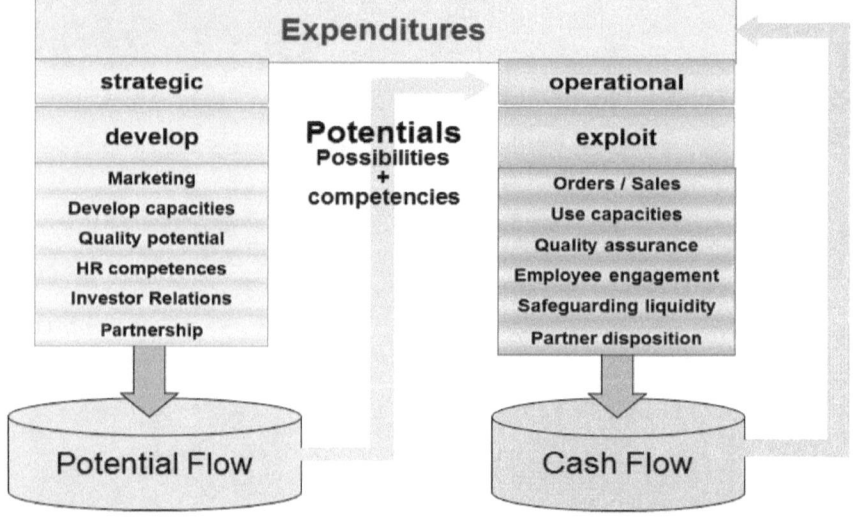

Developing potentials strategically and using them operatively

- "Strategic" means developing new possibilities and capabilities (potentials) which will later (hopefully!) result in monetary inflows. In the meantime "only" potential inflow is realised from that - no cash flow as yet.
- "Operational" signifies the exploitation of existing potentials. Tangible results ensue from that process, and these bring in money in most cases - and we hope that the money received is enough to cover our operational and strategic expenses.

We should measure the objectives of strategic measures with monetary ratios like turnover, profit and capital utilisation only if we are aware that the information we are receiving does not concern the potential inflow.

Example:

Let's consider the (rate) of renewal - the proportion of turnover of new products in total sales. It is used as a measure for strategic objectives in the area of research and development. But what does the renewal rate for the year 2015 tell us?

Let's assume we need 3 years to develop a new product. In that case the renewal rate for 2015 tells us to what extent the research topics we chose in 2012 were the right ones. It does not tell us anything at all about the strategy for the year 2015 - this will only be reflected in the renewal rate of 2018!

So long as we are aware of these delays, the renewal rate is a useful ratio. But if we want to measure the success of strategic research and development work for the year 2015, then this ratio is not appropriate! Instead we could for instance use the number of topics handled and their estimated sales potential as a measure.

If we know from past experience that we must handle ten topics on average in order to strike a win then the measure referred to above could give an important orientation.

2 Conducting a dialogue about strategic objectives

That is not easy; because in the past it was considered an obvious practice the fact that strategic issues were at best discussed within the inner management circles but not with the employees! However this situation changes as soon as the engagement and creativity of the people within the company - executives as well as "ordinary" workers - become essential factors in terms of competition. In such cases a few top executives, no matter how highly qualified they might be, cannot simply dictate the objectives to others because they must fear that they might not be able to hold their ground when competing for the "best heads".

We must therefore allow ourselves to be drawn into the discussion of strategic objectives, for good or for worse. What is more, we shall get used to the fact that we have to lay the assumptions or scenarios, upon which our strategic thoughts are based, "on the table", because every strategy is based on assumptions. After all we don't know what the future holds for us. Hence we also don't know which capabilities will bring success in the future. We can assume, and with reasons, and "be sure" that it will happen that way, based on our experience spanning several years - after all we shall ultimately be left with only assumptions. That's why strategy will only become comprehensible to third parties, if they know these assumptions.

But there is a lot more involved. If we are really to arrive at a common strategy, we have to allow our own assumptions and scenarios to be called into question just as we question other people's assumptions. That requires energy, patience and self confidence, but it is this very approach that will propel us forwards. We shall then be exchanging not just our "opinions" but we shall get into a proper dialogue. Discussions will at best lead to compromises - normally on the smallest common denominator. Dialogue will give all those involved the chance to learn something new and to find a new common level of understanding

That's something which is more than an individual's original considerations.

If on top of that we also get the courage to address our personal ambitions as well as hardships, fears and opposition, which of necessity go with strategic changes, then we shall be able to build trust. And trust is probably the single most important basis for creating changes.

Don´t ever forget:
> Change begins with us ourselves. We have the tendency to promote others and to elevate ourselves as executives above the process. But then, how are we to expect change from others if we don´t work for it ourselves?

Incidentally, readiness to engage in dialogue also leads to tolerance towards mistakes - which is a crucial prerequisite for the capacity to learn. Not in the sense that we should disregard mistakes or that we should underestimate them. But rather, so that we

- Can regard mistakes as a normal occurrence which go hand in hand with progress, and from which we can learn,
- Understand: assumptions are always faulty and incomplete (we cannot "plan" for something unexpected - for example the collapse of Lehman Brothers in 2008!),
- Create an atmosphere in which it is possible to expose mistakes early enough instead of stigmatising them,
- Don't disregard or cover up mistakes, but rather learn to avoid repeating them; only then will the "cost of training" be worthwhile.

> *Ed Land, the creator of the polaroid camera, formulated the meaning of mistakes as follows: "A mistake is an event whose major benefit has not yet worked out to your advantage."*

3 Readiness to shoulder responsibility

Strategy has something to do with the hierarchical or open character of internal structures and the relevant relationships with each other. This has an impact on the Balanced Scorecard too:

- Hierarchies thrive on instructions (commands), on execution (obedience) and on controls (rapport). Open structures of agreements (personal initiative), service (cooperation) and self controlling (consequence).
- In hierarchies, strategic objectives are worked out in the inner management circle then "broken down" to the lower levels and implemented by the subordinates. In open structures, cohesion is based on jointly shared objectives and values as well as on individual readiness to assume responsibility for the drawing up and implementation of those objectives in a team.
- The Balanced Scorecard will also bear hierarchy-like characteristics in hierarchies (objectives, breakdown of objectives, measures, ratios, control reports). Those involved in open structures can do little with the above; they need a Balanced Scorecard for cooperative management with measurable goals.

Principles of "Open Structures"

"Open structures" does not mean the absence of order and responsibility:

- In open structures, management executives are regarded as service providers who organise harmonious work in the organisation. They give "their people" leeway to act independently.
- Staff units and administrative departments become service units which support the execution of tasks by the people - and not to regiment them. In the process, true service will distinguish itself through the fact that it is much sought after and not enforced through "ordinances"!
- The executive directors must also make decisions in open structures - it is not about a wrongly perceived "democracy", but they will have to endeavour to keep their **decisions** transparent, so that they can be understood by the other workers.

In any case "pure theory" does not apply here. In real life you will seldom get a situation where it is "either hierarchy - or openness". Besides, conditions in the individual branches are too varied and experiences with open structures are still minimal. Our interest in the theory therefore is purely thus: we have to decide where to expect the greatest **competitive advantage** from!

And after we have made our decision, the development of a Balanced Scorecard can help us venture and take the first steps on this long and difficult journey towards open structures.

4 Balanced involvement of all stakeholders

"Balanced" in this context means three things:

- On the one hand, that we speak the language of humans, and that this language - with just a few exceptions - is not the language of financial markets. We must formulate our strategy in simple terms so that each person in their daily life can deduce which personal contribution is meaningful. Only what is simple is understandable for all professions!
- On the other hand, balance means placing people's ACTIONS centre stage. To prevent their ACTIONS from resulting into chaos, they need objectives which promote cooperation on their part, and ratios which enable concrete definition of actions as well as the assessment of the course or result of the action.

  Friedag/Schmidt have termed this approach the **"OAR-principle"** (Objective-Action-Ratio):

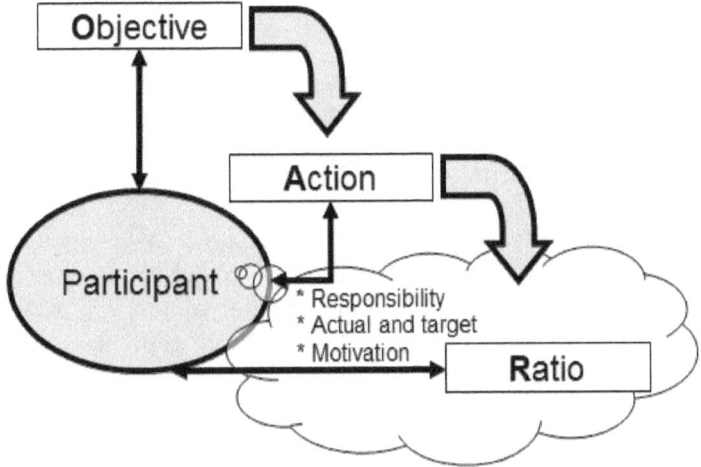

*Management with ratios – the **OAR-principle**[2]*

The OAR-principle does not apply to actions alone. It also applies to every other set goal within the framework of the strategic house, strategic themes, perspectives /development areas, and strategic projects. Due to the need to combine objectives with measurable ratios, we are forced to say exactly what we want to do and what we want to measure ourselves by.

- Lastly the consequent implementation of objectives is part of the aspect of balance. We should not intend to do that which we don´t want or cannot do.

5 Combining simple structures

Since the involvement of people requires simple language, even the structures of a Balanced Scorecard have to be combined in a simple manner. Complex models which can only be understood by a handful of experts are of no use in practical life. People must **understand** which problems are being dealt with. They have to **be able to handle** tasks assigned to them. And they must realise how **important** their ACTIONS will be for themselves and for others - even if "simple" can also mean simplification. As the saying goes: "It is better to be 60% correct than 100% misunderstood!"

---

[2] With oars boats can change direction and reach faster the goal – as companies.

6 Transparency through ratios

In the strategic house (of the management scorecard) emphasis is placed on the transparent organisation of concrete strategic work. That is no easy task, because when assessing potentials - the result of strategic work -we don't have much experience.

The Reporting Scorecard serves to promote the interplay between strategic and operational business. Strategic business is supposed to develop the potentials required for the growth and development of the operational business. The latter must then bring in money which will be used to finance the strategy. This calls for transparent accountability on the part of the people responsible.

7 Concentration on essential issues

Concentration consists in the art of focusing one's attention on one thing. Therefore, concentrating on essential issues means leaving out or postponing that which is less important. The problem does not lie in determining the main focus points but rather in deciding what is to be left out. That requires **consequence**! We shall keep on coming back to this point in subsequent chapters.

At a glance: Introduction to the Balanced Scorecard

- The Balanced Scorecard enables us to develop a tangible strategy and to connect it with objectives which have been formulated in such a way that it is understandable for everybody. It is only then that we can together state what we want to do in concrete terms, in order to achieve our objectives. To achieve that we have to be **simple**.

- The Balanced Scorecard focuses the strategic and operational business on each other. The potentials needed for sustainable success are developed in the strategic business. In the operational business, we have to use the available potentials in such a way that even the strategy can be paid for.

- The Balanced Scorecard can help us to do exactly that which we have set out to do. This is because the strategy is no longer found only on paper, but rather has become an integral part of our actions: Management with measurable goals not only for the benefit of it, but also for the development of potentials. For that to happen, we have to be **consequent**.

- In practice, meanwhile, it has been found that the Balanced Scorecard is suitable not just for industrial firms like Marwitz GmbH, but also for charitable associations or any other organisation.

2   Developing a Balanced Scorecard

Let us now return to our story. In this chapter you will see how the Gutleb-Association finds their strategic orientation and how they use the Balanced Scorecard to translate this strategy into action. We are going to explain to you the meaning of key image and key objective, what strategic coordinates and projects are, and which purpose we are pursuing with the "strategic house".

2.1   Defining General Conditions: our strategy

Time was now ripe for starting working on our Balanced Scorecard. We met in a quiet, lovely little castle in Baden on a sunny Thursday morning, in order to work out our strategy together within three days, as a precondition for a Balanced Scorecard.

We, the four members of the executive team, heads of the two departments of Child and Youth Support and Retirement Homes, two directors from institutions belonging to the two departments, three younger junior staff as well as the chairperson of the workers' council, and Mr. Klaus Marwitz as the representative of the Association's Executive Board. In addition to those we had also invited a representative of the parents and one member of the Advisory Board of the retirement homes, an agile elderly lady of 67 years - we wanted to take into consideration their "perspective" of us. Our small group of strategy formulators consisted of 15 people altogether. To ensure an effective flow of proceedings, we had invited two moderators to conduct the workshop.

A surprise pops up at the beginning

The workshop started with a surprise. We didn't begin with statistical analyses and theoretical deliberations on basic strategic questions. We started by asking each participant to mention the hobbies they practise during their free time, which other activities he/she is involved in apart from his/her profession and family, and what would constitute his/her two most important wishes, which he/she would want to fulfil within the next ten years.

At first I was amazed by that. We had hardly ever spoken about these topics till now. But when the answers started flowing in, we were all surprised and even a bit concerned as to how little we knew of each other – even though we had been working together for so many years. Perhaps it was more of working side by side rather than with each other.

What are the advantages of this personal introductory phase?

I learnt a lot in that one hour - from my colleagues and about them. What a wide spectrum of interests we saw coming to light there! What a series of new connecting factors for personal contact we saw emerging! We can still feel today the impulses which were released during that one hour. They created a "sense of unity" hitherto never experienced in our management team. The way we communicate with each other has become totally different! This has had an extremely positive impact on the work of the association.

As time went by, I have also noticed that those discussions about hobbies, engagements and wishes have influenced the nature of our Balanced Scorecard – at first rather unconsciously but then later in a sustained manner – right up to the time of its practical implementation. In a sense the personal interests and objectives of the members have informed our strategy. Only then has it really become "our strategy".

This whole process was of course not without frustrations. Some of the members had never given any thought to what could be of importance and interest to them in ten years' time. Not everybody was ready to talk about his/her personal wishes and ambitions. However, the largest majority of them went about answering the questions with such openness and naturalness. And the spell which had always hindered exchange of ideas in such gatherings was broken right at the beginning.

The strategic horizon

That was necessary too, because our two moderators asked us in the end to state what we considered to be the special aspects of the Gutleb-Association. We were somewhat irritated by this: I must say that neither I nor my "designated successor" and closest partner in executive management – Jochen Bierath, the "finance chief", Johanna Schranz, the new human resource manager, and Jens Harig, the very young head of purchasing and organisation – could formulate the fundamental objective of the Gutleb-Association or which key objective they are likely to pursue in future.

Of course all members had specific ideas in their heads. But they were nothing more than "headings" or "gut-feelings". And we had not even expressed them – neither among ourselves nor to the other members of the executive team. And definitely not to the wider workers' force. That had gone down in the "daily operational routine".

The issue we addressed was about the strategic horizon, and just like we did when distinguishing between the terms "strategic" and "operational", we usually think exclusively of the temporal horizon in cases like these. However, the contextual objective comes before the time aspect. We must decide the type of relationship we want to set for our fundamental business goal.

For smaller companies or organisations without more pronounced inter-linkages and without considerable future expenditures (e.g. for human resources development, marketing, research & development), the strategic horizon is not too broad. In most cases the immediate experience of "here and now" is enough to safeguard the future, the easily describable forward projection of past experiences with the help of simple assumptions. And should there be serious changes in external conditions, the adjustments are easy to manage. That is just because there are no big inter-linkages to take into account or advance payments to make. However such companies will seldom develop a Balanced Scorecard.

Anyway, this description does not apply to the Gutleb-Association. We are a network of several institutions and furthermore we are integrated into networks of many different partners; we make considerable advance payments - be it investments in new buildings or expenditure for human resources development. An organisation like ours must therefore think outside the box of immediate experiences if it wants to secure its future.

Example:
Factors like demographic development, the development of our social welfare system, and also the economic development of our region and the issues surrounding part-time work are of great strategic importance to the Gutleb-Organisation.

We must try to capture the trends taking place in our community, and which are of relevance to us.

Building up "creative tension" and sustaining it

"And we need profound analyses for that", I interjected. "Why?" one of the moderators asked. "If we are not simply continuing to live in the past but rather want to formulate our goals in such a way that it becomes worthwhile working towards them would it not be better for us then to disengage ourselves, theoretically, from all things past and present? We should remind ourselves of what each one of us wants to achieve in the future and what we as a group want to attain, what role our enterprise is playing in that regard, and where our strengths lie! That is after all the reason why we had asked that question at the beginning of the workshop, rather than talking in abstract terms about the "Gutleb-Association". An organisation on its own does not have goals. In the final analysis, the goal of the organisation is derived from the goals of the people who keep the organisation afloat and work in it."

The moderator pointed out: "Of course anyone can proclaim his own objectives as being those of the organisation, and he might actually be able to push it through. However, chances of his colleagues agreeing to dance to his tune and pulling together with all their might are relatively minimal in the long-run.

But don't forget the analyses in the real sense! For goals alone we achieve little if we do not sharpen the **common** sense of realities at the same time. Only then shall we create the necessary awareness in the entire organisation about the existing gap between goal and reality, and create **common** will to bridge this gap through appropriate actions. It is for this reason that we spoke about the advantages and disadvantages of our competitors, so that we can identify our own strengths and weaknesses".

"And one more thing", he continued, "It is important, for the sake of implementing the decisions, to sustain the common will for change over a long period of time and to resist the pressure of having our goals eroded stealthily." The approach of taking small steps at a time and formulating milestones can be helpful in this regard, provided that we keep an eye on the original strategic goals.

> **Example:**
> The Gutleb-Association wants to develop services for third parties. To achieve that we have to create diverse preconditions; train our employees, introduce marketing activities, etc. It is only after a longer period of time has passed that these efforts will result in extra sales. If we want to motivate our staff, we should work with earlier parameters (e.g. "reactions to a series of marketing advertisements").

"And lastly: We should not forget the fact that money has to be earned from the operational business, and it is with that money that we shall finance our strategy. We should therefore be able to estimate what the strategy will cost, at least roughly, and whether we can afford it - otherwise we shall be creating more frustration than motivation."

Searching for our strategy

We discussed the following situation first in groups and then in a plenary session: society is changing, family networks are breaking up and the state must get involved in issues of raising children. There should be a guaranteed place in nursery schools for every child in our region too. That is a monumental task!

The changes are big even at the other end of life: people become older and they cannot and do not want to be re-homed by the family when they are old and later even become frail.

The cost of providing care is enormous – both in nursery as well as in old people's homes, because the portion of expenditure on human resources is constantly growing.

We were quickly unanimous about these key points. But is that enough for a leading business idea?

Values create identity / solidarity

"Why should people be proud to work in or for the Gutleb-Association?" This question was pinned up in the room. We had never posed it to ourselves in that form and so we dispersed into our groups with some uncertainty to try to answer it. At the beginning it was aspects which we had already formulated in our guidelines that surfaced: "We are an independent, charitable organisation, bound by Christian values, and working for the welfare of children and youths, as well as taking care of the elderly in their old age." That was surely expected.

Only Mrs. Meierke, the representative of the elderly, expressed some reservations: "In that way we shall not be able to get to the crux of the matter. I personally decided to move into the retirement home because I was not just hoping for 'a place to be kept in' but also for 'dignity' in my old age. 'Showing dignity' is for me much more important than Christian values generally. And that applies not only to us or the children but also to the employees!"

That triggered off a lively discussion. Many of the participants made reference to the personal values and expectations which we had talked about at the beginning. By the end we had found three keywords for values which express our identity - the participation in an ethically great task:

- Showing dignity,
- Working together in partnership,
- Independence.

That was perhaps not everything – but it is exactly these aspects that make us stand out.

Our vision – What we strive for

Those discussions got Mrs. Meierke really going now. When we turned to the issue of our vision – the question regarding what we strive for – she began to speak with such vigour: "We should not again begin talking about the less specific formulations from previous years, which could apply to every social institution. I would like to right away suggest something concrete in that respect: Mr. Bierath, you spoke just now about the increasingly difficult financial situation for all social institutions. Why don't we utilise the energy of the often quite hale and hearty elderly people to support child-care services? This was after all how things were in the past within family circles; the old people took care of the children across generations. At the same time the children provided the grandparents with a responsibility. Dignity goes hand in hand with duty within the community, both for us old people and also for the children."

One of the kindergarten teachers disagreed with her: "Do you intend to take away the responsibility of looking after children from the experienced and properly trained members of staff?" "No, I wouldn't like to go that far, but can't we old people read to the children, help them do homework, assist in the kitchen, and once in a while comfort the children? I see how little time you are able to give to the many small problems that the children have! And besides: children also like taking up small responsibilities - like shopping with the granny, going for a walk or surfing the internet with grandpa, making small handicrafts together, etc."

That would be a "win-win-situation", I retorted pensively. The discussion became animated – it was a long evening. And it was only towards midday of the next day that we came up with the following formulation of our now shared vision:

The vision of the Gutleb-Association:

We are an independent, charitable organisation, bound by Christian values, and working for the welfare of children and youths, as well as taking care of the elderly in their old age .

The dignity of man is the main focus of our work:

- We want to impart the basic values of our society to the children and youths in such a way that they embrace them and live according to them.

- The elderly people under our care should be able to spend the last years of their lives in dignity and to a large extent be independent.

- Children and the elderly people live together as partners and support each other and work towards the attainment of a shared living environment in our institutions.

- We want to give our employees room for personal development because only he who has dignity himself can show dignity to others. And the provision of high quality care requires motivated workers.

After those deliberations we then dealt with the more fundamental aspects of translating our drafted vision into something practical. What are the strategic challenges that we must be ready to face? How can we achieve "engagement with dignity"?

One thing was clear: It was necessary to structure our institutions differently, both in terms of business processes and also physical structures, in order to create room for cross-generational engagement. How much internal motivation was required for us to accomplish that goal using our own resources?

Our Mission – Whom we are there for

We have discussed a lot about our social duty, which is supposed to give us energy to implement the necessary changes. We then came to the following common view regarding our actions:

The mission of the Gutleb-Association:

"Through our engagement spanning different generations,
we give dignity to the people under our care –
because we give our employees dignity and
the opportunity to grow in this task:
personal responsibility, supportive business processes and suitable
room to operate in".

With that formulation we had determined the persons whom we are there for. The cornerstones of our business ideal – identity/values, vision and mission - had now been laid.

Our core expertise

We then turned to an issue whose practical importance I only understood properly much later. That was the issue regarding our core benefit. What makes our products and services marketable?

- Products and services on their own have no value as yet – they must be turned into a good for the people who are supposed to buy it. As one beautiful saying goes: "The bait is for the fish to like, not the fisherman".

- However, that is not enough. We must test to find out which price is appropriate for the good. The "desire" for the good must always be somewhat greater than the "pain" of the price to be paid.

- The price has another limitation – "allowed" costs. The tension between the good and the price must make it possible to realize sales (price x turnover) which in turn enables sufficient development of the necessary capabilities and processes, including marketing and servicing of all our financial obligations.

We need a balanced relationship between product, good, price and allowed costs. Unilateral considerations endanger our understanding of business and market forces.

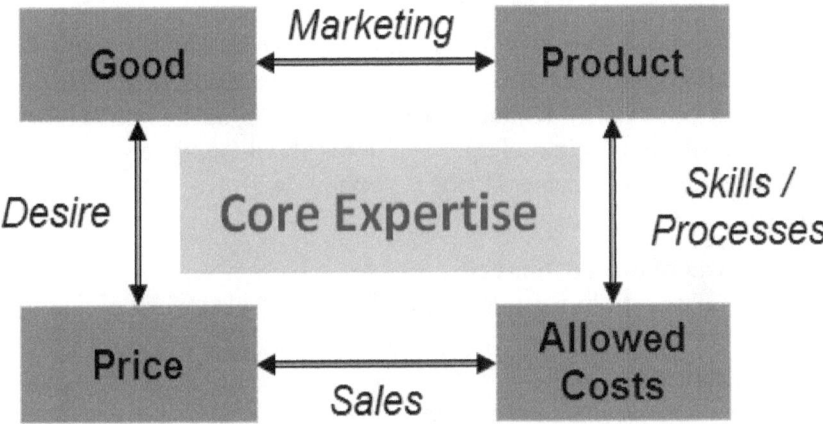

The core expertise describes the marketability of the business idea

We were not accustomed to this way of viewing the core of our service delivery; and certainly not to the issue of allowed costs. "We are indeed good and money does not matter to us." That is something for the "profit-oriented" – not for us.

However, Mr. Bierath was the first person to make us learn that this "ideal world" has never existed in that form. Our eyes had only been closed to reality. It was high time we opened them. We must always ask ourselves the two questions: How do we want to live – and in that process we view work as an important part of our life – and how do we intend to finance that life?

Now we turn to our core expertise. I wouldn't want to bore you with details of our discussions. Finally we had found initial access to "the core":

Time for personal attention
This is actually what makes us stand out. The issue now was to find ways and means of bringing it about in a more cost-effective manner than before. That is going to keep us busy in the coming years. Can we guarantee enough "time for personal attention" and at the same time operate economically? Can we assert ourselves on the market of social support services even in the future? Does this business idea support our business?

The Gutleb-Business Model

The next morning was devoted to drafting our business model. Even though Gutleb has an advantage over the usual businesses, in that it does not have to make profit, its business operations still have to be paid for.

I had already reported in more general terms about the major components used to build our business model. Specifically we worked out the following aspects:

- **The needs of our customers:**
  Humaneness – to live in dignity in old age and also when giving child care.
- **Our target customers:**
  Children/adolescents between three and twelve years of age, as well as people who do not want to feel rejected in their old age in a community governed by Christian values.
- **Our core competences:**
  We promote and demand engagement, and we give dignity, thanks to the values of our employees.
- **Our uniqueness:**
  cross-generational engagement for dignified life in a Christian-oriented environment.

We saw a big enough sales and margin potential in this constellation: The market is there and continues to grow thanks to policy guidelines, changes in family setup and the higher life expectancy. Given the engagement of our customers and that of the association members, we can afford not just to give dignity, but also to operate in a cost-effective manner. Besides, we shall occupy a special position in our region. We are all convinced of that in our hearts.

Agenda 2025

We had not yet come to the end of the workshop, though. "If that is to be Gutleb's key business idea, of which "magnitude" should it be then?" - the moderators asked. "What are the future perceptions of the organisation's board of directors?"

I had previously agreed on our company's policy orientation with the executive:

- Safeguarding financial independence
- Moderate growth using our own resources
- Increasing the workforce to about 3,000 employees within the next 10 years
- Safeguarding our substantive work areas.

This was supposed to pass through as the first statement of "Agenda 2025". We had not yet envisaged anything more than this. So we did a little brainstorming. How many places and what revenue would be conceivable with 3,000 employees? This was admittedly just a gut-feeling, but coupled with "my people's" experience, this was already an orientation too:

	Today	2025
Places for children:	6,000	13,500
Places for old people:	2,500	5,500
Revenue:	83 M€	201 M€

Strategic components

Allow me to deviate a little. Basing on the results of the workshop, we sat down together during the weeks after and worked out the first broad scenario for 2025, an initial projection and nothing more:

scenario 2025		Children	Senior citizens	Admin.	Total
Places		13,500	5,500		
Utilisation level	%	95	97		
Employees		920	2,000	80	3,000
Investments	k€/a	8	3		4
Salaries/SV	k€/a	26	50	4	79
Material costs	k€/a	12	100	5	117
∑ Expenditure	k€/a	38	153	9	200
Revenue	k€/a	39	162		201
Cash Flow*	k€/a	1	9	-9	1

* Cash Flow = payment surpluses or deficits

This should then be turned into precise steps and concretised in milestones (2016-2017; 2018-2020; and later). Despite all "approximations" this seems to me to be a suitable guideline for our subsequent course of action.

Topic pool and focus

Now back to the workshop. We now had a business idea, our core expertise, the business model and an Agenda 2025. To conclude this first workshop, we collected important topics which we wanted to deal with in the coming years – from a retrospective point of view – in order to translate our strategy into action. And in order not to lose track of what we were doing, we gave this topic pool a structure (I have inserted here a few selected examples):

Management	Products
- Quality of care	- Services for third parties
- "Harmony" of disciplines and departments	- Develop the "Modern Senior Citizens" programme
- Combining family and profession	- Social fitness for children and youths
- Systematic health promotion	- Structural changes
Communication	**Organisation**
- Structure communication	- Growth of membership in the association
- Talk more intensely with one another instead of about one another	- Harmonise processes
	- Centralised vs. decentralised organisation of work
- Company glossary	- Analyse performance ("Reduce wastage")

Lastly, together we spread out the topics on a timeframe from 2015 – 2025. That produced an initial diagram showing which tasks we wanted to start when.

We then came to a "satisfactory conclusion". Although the past three days had been very stressful for us all, there was a remarkably good feeling among the participants. No one had expected so many discussions. However, we could now start building a common image for our future and then during the next workshop – seven weeks later - embark on plans for its concrete implementation.

> *This kind of preliminary work for a concept and for the development of a strategy is necessary but not sufficient yet! Because the rather comprehensive strategic goals must be implemented, that means they have to be translated into concrete objectives and concrete actions. That is the work of the Balanced Scorecard."*

2.2   Developing a Balanced Scorecard in Seven Steps

The general framework was now established. We met for the second workshop and could now turn to the implementation of the strategy, and hence to the "actual" Balanced Scorecard. We are going to follow seven steps:

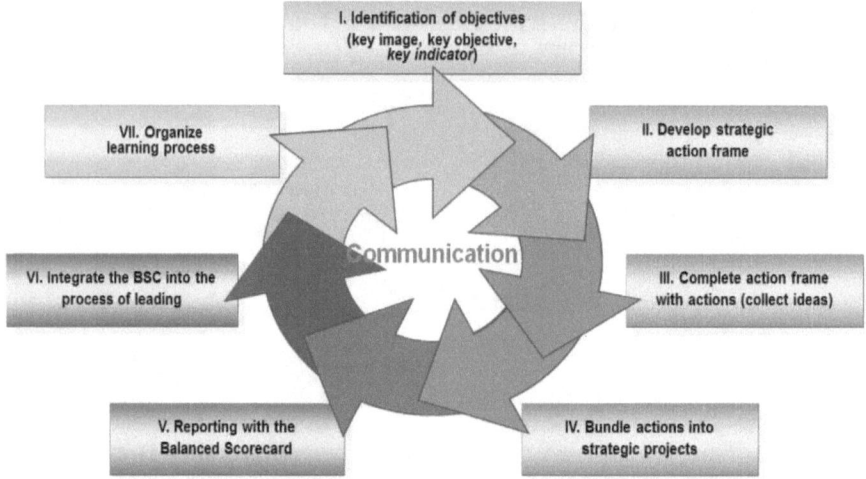

Seven steps for the development of a Balanced Scorecard

Determining the time frame

"We shall discuss with you in the next three days what you *now* need to concentrate on, what you *now* want to set about on in order to implement your business idea step by step. It is true you have formulated the Agenda 2025 and the strategic topic pool, but you must now derive very specific tasks from them, with which you can immediately begin. If in that process we think 18 months ahead, that will already be a lot, because we cannot right now get an overview of the constellations which will be significant for us at later stages"; that's how the moderators opened the session. "Therefore let us talk about the period 2015/2016." That was an important way of focusing. The longer the time frames, the less binding the target projections will be. And reliability was our weak point.

2.3   Step 1: Key image and key objective

With that introduction we started with the first group session of our second workshop. We were given the assignment to name and give reasons for the

- Key image and
- Key objective

of the Gutleb-Association for the next 18 months.

During that process we were supposed to show both the link between those two concepts and the business idea and also the relationship between key image and key objective.

The key image – how our company is viewed

By key image – derived from or in the course of formulating the mission statement – we mean the picture which people shall develop about us in the next 18 months.

- What could entice the customers to spend their money just on our services?
- What do our customers, suppliers or employees use to measure their success – with regard to the services offered by us?

If we succeed in credibly conveying the fact that we help people to be successful, and telling them why we can do it better than our competitors, then we shall have already won – as long as we are also able to keep our promises.

After some discussion the key image had taken on the following outlines:

> **Key image of Gutleb-Association:**
> Care is more than a profession to us.
> „Gutleb – Engagement with Dignity"

All our customers and partners should know the following: For us, the dignity of a human being is not only an ethical principle, but also common practice. For that we promote and demand engagement. That is a big challenge, especially to the employees and members of Gutleb-Association, and also to our customers. But we are confident that we will fulfil it in future. At the very least we will embark on the journey to that goal.

Supporting our identity with a Logo

We also had a first idea for a new logo, with which we wanted to announce our changed perspective on the market. This logo – which is of course being designed by a graphics company – is meant to send our message to all potential partners in the region, customers as well as suppliers, policy makers and the general public:

Our idea of a new logo for the Gutleb-Association

The key objective – what we want to achieve

With regard to the inwardly focused key objective – derived from or in the process of formulating the vision of the company - we shall agree on what we want to be considered as the crucial potential for future sustainability of our business in the next 18 months and what we want to expand. We must of course convey that message to all employees in a comprehensible manner. Three questions have to be answered:

- What is necessary for us to maintain our presence in the market?
- What is (personally) desirable?
- What is feasible in the Gutleb-Association?

In connection with the key objective, we were first given the task of defining a (key) ratio: What shall we use to measure our success? And only one (!) ratio, so that we can answer the question:

"Why are we **one** enterprise?"

We argued for a long time about the formulation of our key objective. Finally we came to the following assessment: Our economic success depends on how we shall manage to promote cross-generational engagement. This is particularly the case with regard to our employees who should not view it as an encroachment on their field of work, but rather as a chance to show more human feeling in their dealings with each other. That also applies to our customers, children as well as elderly people, whom we want to induce to attain dignity through engagement. It is only by so doing that we shall be able to achieve healthy growth. We therefore made the following postulation:

> **Key objective of Gutleb-Association:**
> We shall allow room for cross-generational engagement.

> **Key indicator of Gutleb-Association:**
> *Number of participating customers [#]*

With that formulation[3] we had created a roof for our "Strategic House":

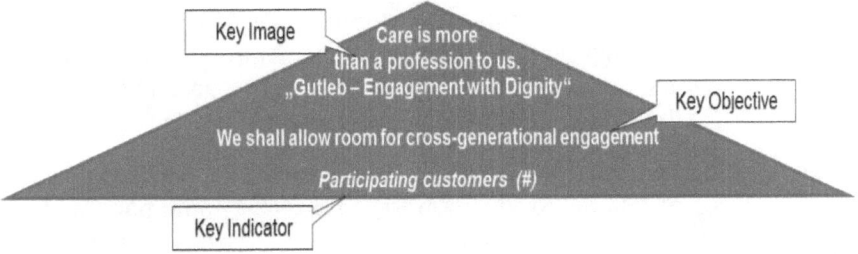

The roof of the "Strategic Gutleb-House"

---

[3] The respective number is symbolised here by „#"

2.4   Step 2: Strategic coordinate system

The key image and key objective were the first step towards our Balanced Scorecard. The next task was to concretise them and to define the objective, content and ratio of the

- Strategic topics and
- Development areas for building up potentials
  (or perspectives – as Kaplan/ Norton put it)

That leads to the creation of a target system which describes quite precisely, what we actually want to attain with our strategy and which consequences we expect to encounter.

> *This target system too is – like all the others – nothing more than a combination of assumptions. However, we shall make those assumptions transparent and hence comprehensible for the people in the company.*
> *That is the crucial factor.*

Strategic topics

We want to use the strategic topics to determine the other part-objectives which we all consider to be essential for making our key objective possible. The topic pool can be of help to us in that regard; and we should also concretise the strategic topics with adequate ratios!

When working on these topics the steps should not be too big. If we want the employees of Gutleb-Association to move at the same pace with us, then we must pick them up from where they are at the moment. That requires us to measure the strategic topics in such a way that everybody can follow.

> *There is an English proverb which says: "One should only jump over the fence when one is right in front of it. However, practicing how to jump can be done elsewhere."*

Therefore we deliberated on what decisions we have to take now or those that will "become due" much later.

In the end we had agreed on three strategic topics, again with an objective and a ratio:

- Strategic topic 1 (T1): Quality of care
- Strategic topic 2 (T2): Growth in membership
- Strategic topic 3 (T3): Services for third parties

Our house was continuing to take on new features:

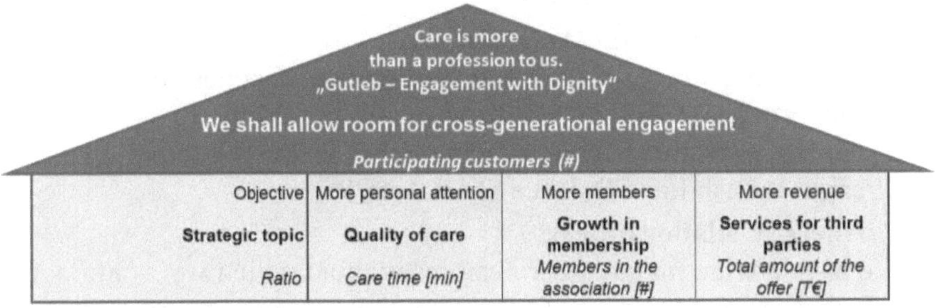

The following content appears within the house diagram:

Care is more
than a profession to us.
„Gutleb – Engagement with Dignity"

We shall allow room for cross-generational engagement

Participating customers (#)

Objective	More personal attention	More members	More revenue
Strategic topic	Quality of care	Growth in membership	Services for third parties
Ratio	Care time [min]	Members in the association [#]	Total amount of the offer [T€]

The "Gutleb-House" is growing

Our stakeholders' perspectives

After the lunch-break we started deliberating on the question: Which potentials do we want to develop in order to be able to successfully tackle the strategic topics for the realization of the key image and key objective? And whom we need in the boat for that task?

- **Customers:**
  Our strategic position is influenced considerably by the engagement of our target group (children or occupants of our homes respectively). We assume that the dignity of the people will benefit from this engagement. This will translate into a better reputation for our institutions and subsequently into demand for our services. We can measure that by the "number of people on our waiting lists".

- **Employees:**
  Without competent and flexible employees we don't stand a chance of making ourselves relevant in the future. Our main goal for this area of development is to attain flexibility, to work with a diverse and committed group of people, to be ready to take a back seat and to question established procedures. To achieve this we have to train our employees even more intensively than before. The "number of training days" is therefore supposed to guide us as a ratio along the path to more flexibility among our workers.

- **Finances (Pillars of the Association):**
  The independence of the Gutleb-Association depends directly on its creditworthiness, and by implication on its ability to mobilise the resources it requires. One suitable ratio is the "Internal Financial Strength" (Cash Flow/Balance Sheet Total)".

- **Partners (Collaborations):**
  We have a wide range of partnerships without which we would not be able to carry out our work. At the same time, we have to ensure that our partners also support our key image. In that connection we want to subject them to an "internal rating" and to keep the "proportion of A-partners" as high as possible.

- **(Policy towards the) local government:**
  It is advantageous for a charitable organisation like ours to forge good relationships on the political arena. We can achieve that by making contacts with key players in local and regional politics. The "number of meetings with local politicians" should serve as an appropriate ratio for us.

The target system was now accomplished.

We had agreed on a key image and the key objective for the Gutleb-Association.

We had now developed our coordinate system based on that:

1 We had determined the strategic topics that are relevant for the attainment of our goals.

2 And we had taken a critical look at our network of relationships (perspectives) with the aim of finding out which potentials were particularly well suited to be developed further, and with which interest groups (stakeholders), in order to attain our key objective as effectively as possible.

		Care is more than a profession to us. „Gutleb – Engagement with Dignity"		
		We shall allow room for cross-generational engagement		
		Participating customers (#)		
	Objective	More personal attention	More members	More revenue
	Strategic topic	Quality of care	Growth in membership	Services for third parties
	Ratio	Care time [min]	Members in the association [#]	Total amount of the offer [T€]
Perspectives	Engagement **Customer** Waiting list [#]			
	Flexibility **Employees** Training [d]			
	Creditworthiness **Finances** Internal financial strength [T€]			
	Support of our key image **Partner** A-partners [%]			
	Contacts **Local Government** # Meetings			

The outlines of the "Strategic Gutleb-House"

The system of assumptions which forms the basis for our strategic action is now illustrated in a manner that is comprehensible to all. We shall check all ideas geared at strategic actions for their adaptability to our house.

2.5   Step 3: Strategy-focused actions

A house needs to be inhabited. We must populate it, and that means populating it with ideas for concrete, targeted actions. It is only our actions that will breathe life into the strategy.

We then set about "looking for ideas". We were of course aware of the fact that concentration on just a few strategic topics, narrowing of developmental areas to specific aspects, leaves certain things unattended to, which can also lead to success. However, the longstanding experience of our strategy team had led us to believe that we can, with good conscience, live with these limitations.

We cannot do everything, just as we cannot finance everything! But the choice of our actions should as much as possible be made consciously and according to jointly agreed criteria. And we had defined these criteria with the "house" as the action framework, our strategic coordinates.

There were of course a thousand ideas swirling around in our heads when we – again in small groups – were instructed to note down on our moderation cards everything which was to be tackled.

OAR – Objective, Action, measurable **Ratio**

Prior to that, our moderators had sworn us to the fact that we also had to determine the objective of every action which was to be attained. To put it even more clearly: first comes the objective and then comes reflection on what exactly must be done! And then lastly a ratio which was to either provide information about the progress of our practical actions (more of an early ratio), or one which assesses the attainment of our goals (a late ratio). **O**bjective - **A**ction - measurable **R**atio is what the moderators called this method - the OAR-principle (oar = a long stick with a wide flat blade at one end, used for rowing a boat – and we have to row daily!). And the actions have yet to be fitted into the strategic coordinate system:

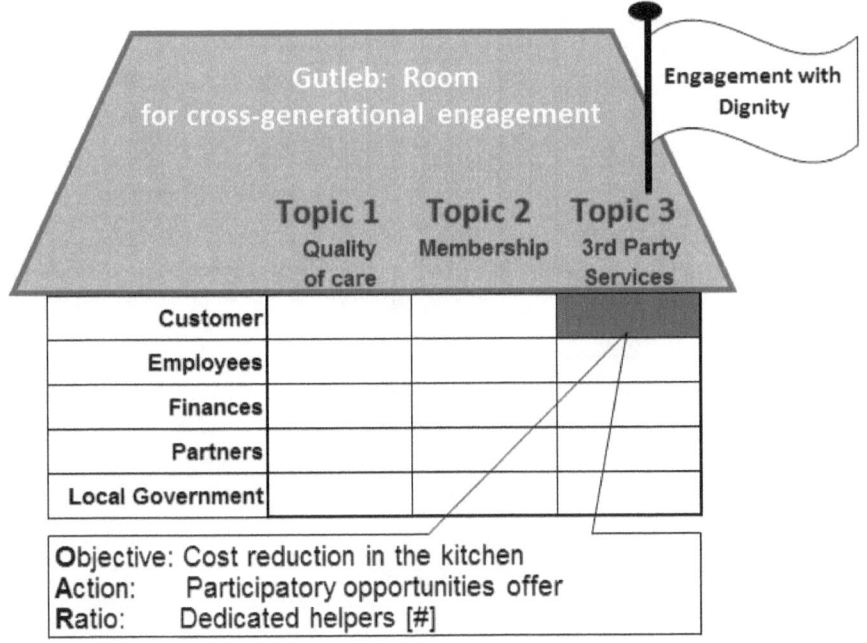

	Topic 1 Quality of care	Topic 2 Membership	Topic 3 3rd Party Services
Customer			
Employees			
Finances			
Partners			
Local Government			

Objective: Cost reduction in the kitchen
Action: Participatory opportunities offer
Ratio: Dedicated helpers [#]

Assignment of Strategic Actions

That was a bit too much for the initial stage. But after the opening moments of uncertainty and successful handling the customers perspectives, we became more and more creative; each group created between three and eight ideas per development area for targeted actions or better still: OAR.

We then went into a plenary session where we discussed the various ideas which we had generated in our small groups. Needless to say, some of them were like "water that had already flowed under the bridge". We were already implementing them (why wasn't everybody seeing that? – the thought rumbled in my head!). I had also already discussed some of the other ideas with one or the other colleague. But a lot of those ideas were actually new, never before talked about, discussed, rejected or accepted by us. And some proposals were downright quite revolutionary; they opened up completely new aspects for our work.

During the discussions, our moderators insisted on describing why the proposed actions met the demands of our strategic house. Some proposals were then dropped and set aside. However, the discussion did bring some new insights too.

> *Similar proposals for strategic actions should be accepted if they describe different facets of a given problem in an analogous manner. What is essential is to note down in very concrete terms what has to be done. In that process, "similar ideas" can hardly be avoided.*
>
> *On the other hand, actions which are described using terms like "improve", "replace", "optimise" or "concentrate" should not be adopted, or if at all then only in a modified form. Such concepts describe everything or nothing, and they therefore don't give any concrete orientation.*

The interesting thing was that very few proposals revolving around far distant things (in terms of time) were raised; most of the action ideas showed obvious courses of action for each of us. Apparently we were all ready to take our future into our own hands right now, and not wait until three or five years later.

Our target system had given us something to orientate ourselves by in future. But we were once again back to the present with the aim of determining which actions we needed to improve our capabilities, our potentials, in order to realise that future. It was only by doing so that it now became clear to us, what our target orientation means in concrete terms, and what very immediate demands result from it; demands not only on other people, on our employees and partners, but also on us personally – the executive directors of the Gutleb-Association!

A group-dynamic process

By the time we finished we had collected well over 100 different ideas for strategic actions. Each of us had ideas scribbled on action cards, and these were then presented by the respective groups during the plenary session. Each group of course fought hard to defend their ideas, and they tried to convince the rest of us why their ideas complied with the strategic requirements. We witnessed the emergence of true team spirit within the various groups, but thanks to the ever changing membership of the small groups, it did not result in the creation of the "us against them" feeling. Due to the intensive discussions, it was always our ideas, our creation, our future, which we wanted to tackle. There was also a bit of "euphoria" regarding all those ideas we had managed to assemble.

Selected OAR-Examples

The "Action-Day" was crowned with a delicious dinner, and the red "Viertele" wine from Baden soon made us drop to our beds with exhaustion. However, sleep was the last thing on my mind. There were many thoughts turning in my head. I therefore once again flipped through some of those OAR-cards in my mind, which were particularly important to me. I structured some action ideas which I thought were outstanding according to the selected strategic coordinates and pondered over them.

The employee-development area

Let us remind ourselves of the employees perspective:

Objective:	To improve the flexibility of the employees
Perspective:	Employees
Ratio:	*Training days [#]*

I would like to introduce four OAR-examples which, on the one hand, all lead to the strengthening of our workers' flexibility in the company, so that we can give our "part-time" employees, young and old, many opportunities for engagement. On the other hand, the strategic topics should at the same time be supported.

Example: Actions for strategic topic T1

Objective T1:	Better care by giving more attention
Strategic topic T1:	To improve the quality of care
Ratio T1:	*Amount of care time used [min]*

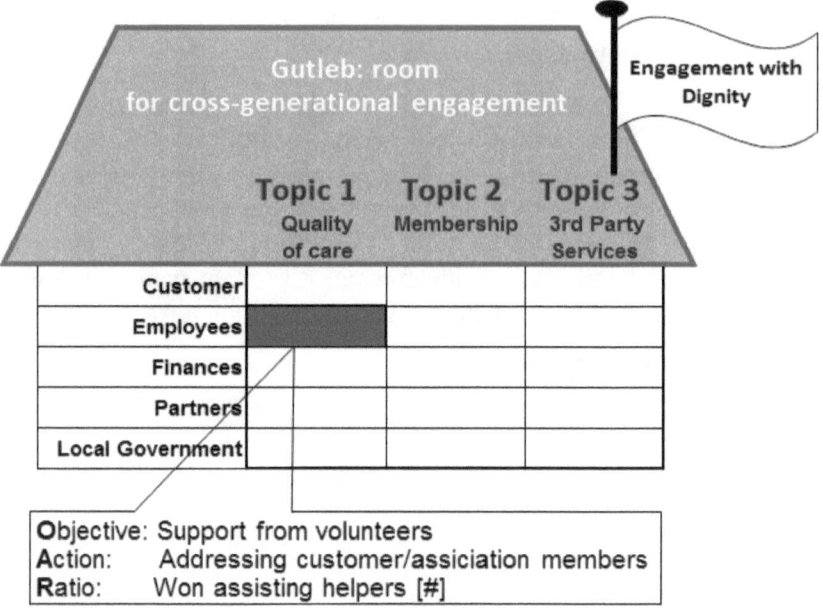

	Topic 1 Quality of care	Topic 2 Membership	Topic 3 3rd Party Services
Customer			
Employees			
Finances			
Partners			
Local Government			

Objective: Support from volunteers
Action: Addressing customer/assiciation members
Ratio: Won assisting helpers [#]

Address customer/association members

Background

We would like to not only offer our clients, both juniors and seniors, care which is as comprehensive as possible but also to impart to them dignity through engagement.

That requires time and costs money. On the other hand, clients such as those we have in our organisation are a big pool of potential voluntary workers who are always ready to help and whom we should engage so that they can support us in our work.

This address is not meant to be striking; the employees are supposed to be trained to take the initiative and to inspire customers/ members of the organisation for practical tasks at hand within their surroundings. In that way we shall at the same time be promoting the spirit of engagement among our employees, because through that, they too will get time for (more) important assignments.

Measurement process

We shall record the number of voluntary workers.

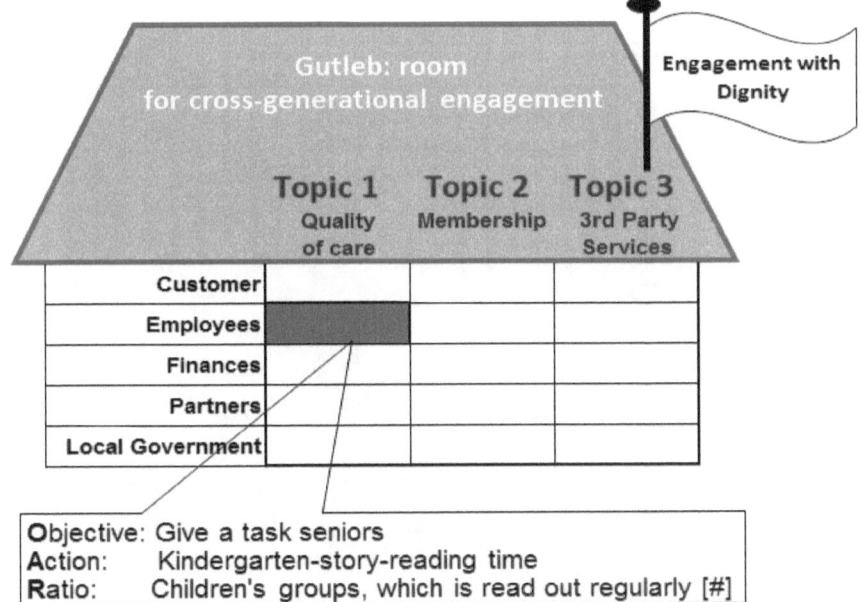

Kindergarten-story-reading time

Background

Who has never experienced such a scenario: Elderly people, particularly those living in retirement homes, are on the scrap heap. But why is that so? Can't an elderly person maybe take a book and read it to children in a nursery school next door? Or indeed help in the kitchen and even carry out other wide-ranging duties, be active and feel challenged? And through that, obtain dignity?

I got to know an institution for critically disabled people in Vienna, who all had a task in their group or for the parent organisation, commensurate with the gravity of their disability. Those people were glad not to be rejected and on top of that they were earning some money for themselves, while also reducing the expenses of the parent organisation.

We wanted to address that issue actively. Not for the sake of saving money, but with the aim of giving our senior citizens a meaningful assignment of imparting the value of reading books to the children and relieving our employees.

Measurement process

We count the children's groups in which public readings take place regularly.

Example: Action for strategic topic T2

Objective T2:	Success by more members for the organisation
Strategic topic T2:	Growth in membership
Ratio T2:	*Number of members [#]*

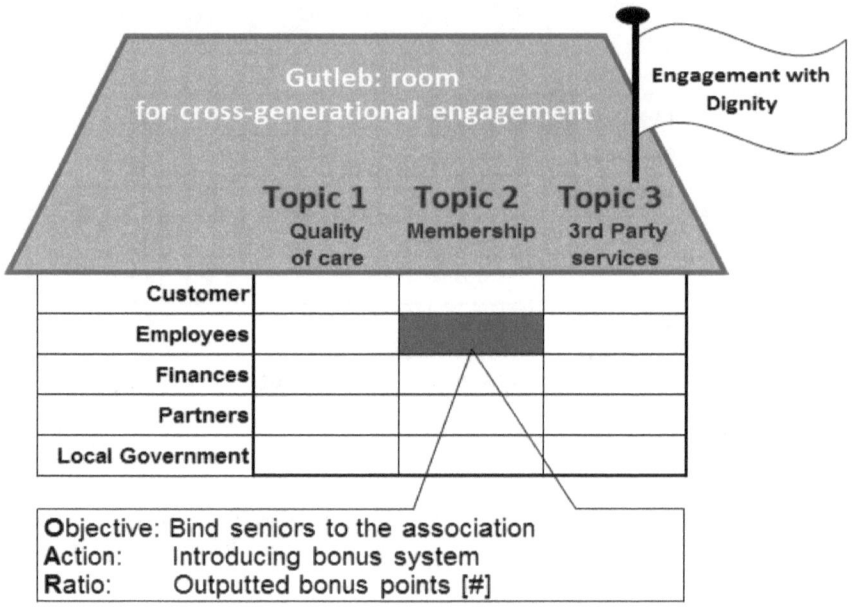

Introducing the bonus system

Background

Our organisation thrives on the commitment of its members and sponsors. And commitment in this case mainly means work, voluntary services in and for our institutions. Those services should be rewarded, because then we can also demand services more regularly. However, we don't intend to pay for those services but rather to compensate for them using bonus points.

Those bonus points will determine the order of ranking in our waiting list for the elderly, among other things, and it will also give one privileges in the selection of rooms as well as choices for grandchildren in nursery school.

In that way, employees will get more time for training or to get used to other business processes.

Measurement process
For each one hour of work, one bonus point will be awarded; if the work is done with a lot of commitment, double points are given – though the directors of the institutions are allowed to award only 25% double points. The points given out are recorded.

Example: Action for strategic topic T3

Objective T3:   Additional income through services delivered
Strategic topic T3: Services for 3rd parties
Ratio T3:   *Total amount of the offer (k€) - early ratio or*
                   agreed sum of the contract (k€) - late ratio

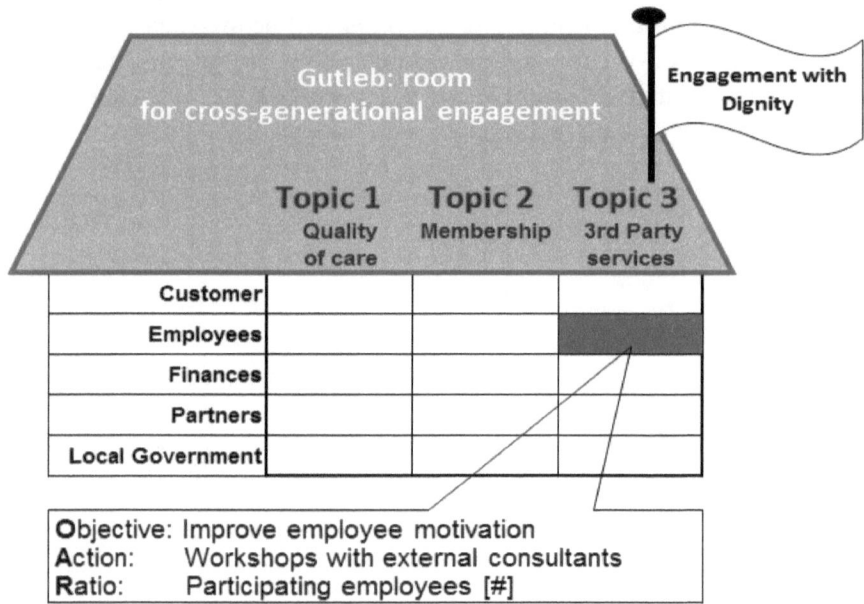

Workshops with external consultants

Background

I have just read a research study of one big German enterprise in which it was stated that motivation of the workers is not only significant but also considerably higher if they are involved in drawing up the definition of the objective.

That is actually common sense, but how many companies still apply the top-down approach, which then makes the workers unmotivated.

And then we start asking questions when the expected results are not realised, when flexibility, readiness and creativity which are necessary for our times are lacking in our employees.

Isn't that partly the case with us too? Shouldn't we open up too - No, must we not open up?

Together with the external advisors and moderators, we therefore want to learn how to make our employees more involved in utilising the know-how and the certainly available commitment.

We want to define our goals together, in the way we started doing it today - but that does not mean that everyone does their own thing, but instead that we should think in our respective teams about what we can do (rather than always leaving it to others), basing that on our business idea and our key objective. In that case the employees should be called upon to think, to generate ideas as to how we can use our know-how on the market even better, that is to say not only for our institutions.

We have to reduce our costs too. That can be done by reducing the costs themselves or by providing more service at the same cost. (Why do most managers have a narrow view of the future which is biased towards the formula of cost reduction = laying off workers?)

Measurement process
The number of workers who take part in the relevant workshops.

We of course generated many more ideas than those described in the employee development area above. However, I wanted to show that we tried as much as possible to describe concrete tasks which we assumed would improve our potentials. And so I gradually became at peace with myself and went to sleep...

Digression: Early and Late ratios

Both early and late ratios measure past performance - nobody can measure things in the future. But we have assumptions in our minds about many of the ratios - assumptions from which we draw conclusions about the future. We have, for instance, learnt that a high number of offers is an early ratio of later orders. Must that always be the case? And does your partner understand this chain of assumptions?

> *Disclose your assumptions for the so- called early ratios and communicate this chain! In that way, every ratio could actually be an early ratio. Within the framework of a Balanced Scorecard, you should work in a balanced way with early and late ratios.*

2.6   Step 4: Bundling and implementing projects

I dreamt a lot at night, and I even had a nightmare: I saw myself surrounded by hundreds of colourful cards which were all collapsing on me saying "I", "I", "I". Were we asking too much of ourselves? Everything at the same time? Won't the operational work come off badly in the process?

I must have had a pretty restless night and I decided to express my fears to one of the moderators at breakfast. He smiled and said with a grin: "Even Karlsruhe was not built in one day - we'll cross that bridge when we come to it."

The time came faster than we had anticipated: Right after breakfast we were standing at two empty boards which formed a frame around our two "OAR-boards". "What belongs together, should grow together", the moderator said and requested all of us to go in front and put all those OAR-cards which belonged together into one group.

Bundling of Actions

"Come on!" We stood clueless in front of the boards, and studied the OAR-cards described yesterday (and became annoyed about the handwriting of one or the other member). It took time and questioning glances directed at the moderator, but we soon became at ease and realized: "This idea goes together with the other OAR-card!" We therefore re-grouped all the cards, one by one, until only three remained.

During that process one of us was given the task of giving names to the various groups which had been created. Eight project ideas emerged.

Then one of the moderators grabbed the sceptre again. To check whether the assignment of ideas to the cards was appropriate, he requested one of us at a time to once again read out the cards, one by one. Given such a chaotic grouping of cards, it was no surprise that we now and again discovered some OAR-cards which, in terms of meaning, belonged to a different project idea. We got rid of one project idea completely; the cards under it fitted more to other project ideas. And our three remained OAR-cards also found somewhere to belong. Our final result was as follows:

Strategic projects of Gutleb - Association

- Project 1: Encouragement for senior citizens
- Project 2: Structural adjustment
- Project 3: Further training
- Project 4: Financial power
- Project 5: Services
- Project 6: Regional cooperation
- Project 7: Engagement for the youth

Review of strategic projects

We had seven strategic project ideas which had to be worked on. A project like this looked like a chicken with plucked feathers - incomplete and hard to "enjoy". The moderators then explained to us the seven steps for designing concrete, workable and implement able projects from the project ideas generated by us:

1 Formation of a work group

One participant at a time from our management team assumed the role of temporary project leader, a so-called patron, for purposes of working on a project. It was his duty to choose two colleagues to assist him and to draw up the structure of his project within the next seven weeks.

> *Use this chance to open up your company's structure a little. As a project leader, one should choose persons who are not working in the same department where the main focus of the strategic project lies. The technical expertise from the department concerned must of course be represented in the team, but whenever possible not as a project leader - otherwise you will miss the opportunity to, on the one hand, have more understanding among yourselves, and on the other hand to consequently implement new ideas.*

Example:
> In a logistics project, a sales employee for instance, would be a worthwhile temporary project leader, but for a marketing project, someone from the production department would be a better choice.

2 Setting the project goal

What do we really want to achieve with the proposed strategic project? What does the common denominator of the grouped OAR-cards consist in? These things should be defined and formulated using a clear project objective. This objective must fit into the strategic coordinate system.

3 Defining the project ratio

We had already experienced this before: A ratio helps us to capture the objective described in words more accurately and to assess its correct implementation later.

Therefore, the starting point, the objective and possibly the individual milestones, must be determined for each project. Those milestones are - after their confirmation by the management board of the company - the target areas for the project leader, for which he is responsible. We therefore have an objective, a project name and a ratio for each strategic project - just like for the strategic coordinates and actions.

Example: strategic project "Financial strength"	
Objective: Safeguard independence by strengthening the organisation's activities Project: Financial strength Ratio: Total amount donated [k€]	
O: Secure the loyalty of potential customers A: Build up "mixed hiking groups" R: Participants [#]	O: Secure the loyalty of the target group A: Determine the bonus performance R: Working with bonus points [#]
O: Secure the loyalty of potential customers A: Introduce bonus system for performance R: Bonus points [#]	O: Win members A: Joint activities R: New members of the organisation [#]
O: Address target groups/media A: Open day R: Participants [#]	O: Members buy from partners A: Cheque-book for partners R: Used cheque-books [#]
O: Development offers A: Joint creative workshops R: Offers [#]	O: Joint offers A: Create a joint sales agency R: Joint offers [#]
O: A-Partners as members A: Surcharge preference for members R: A-Partners [#]	O: Members as multipliers A: Information about donations for members R: Total amount donated [k€]

Project "Financial strength"

4 Widening the project structure

The actions were developed purposefully in order to meet the strategic coordinates. None of us had even thought of strategic projects during that process. Now the projects had to be made broader with more actions, probably now better described as "project steps".

Are they ten or fifty project steps all together? That depends on the size of the company and that of the project. However, a tangible number of project steps are recommended in that case too, although you will perhaps break down steps which are closest in terms of time into more refined steps which should be captured rather roughly in the distant future.

If the strategic project is large scaled, it will easily lose manageability. One can then tinker with the idea of applying the system of the Balanced Scorecard on a strategic project too. For such big projects, one can form a project group of 10 to 15 experts from all sections of the company. We shall then structure the project in an analogous manner with a project objective (Key objective of the project) and strategic coordinates. Actions aimed at particular goals are then worked out in a brainstorming session and summarised into partial projects, of course with an objective and ratio respectively.

5 The chronological order of the project steps

Not everything must of course be accomplished immediately and at the same time in a project; some things require more time and others less time. Some of them overlap - accomplishment of various steps is also the precondition for starting another project step.

6 Assessing the required resources

This is not about being accurate to the last cent but the magnitude of the costs should already be known before one decides to implement a project.

Costs do not only refer to running costs but also to cost effective investments and the utilisation of time by our employees for project related work.

By combining the chronological sequence and the resource needs we can estimate the cash flow of the project through its entire lifetime and this is a precondition for taking the project to the planning stage.

7 Assessing the impact on the strategic coordinate system

Entrepreneurial activities are too complex to be described in formulae. There are hardly any linear dependencies in real life; they are too simplistic and they don't allow us to believe in non-existent accuracies. But one should nevertheless explain the effects which the strategic project will have on our target system.

For each of the matrix elements from strategic topics and perspectives we shall examine the effects which the project progress has: good (+2), rather positive (+1), none (0), rather negative (-1) or bad (-2). In this way we will be able to establish the degree of intensity with which we shall work on the individual development areas. One could of course refine this structure even further, but from our experience, that does not add any meaningfulness.

In the example of the Gutleb-Association with its 15 development areas, each project can attain a maximum value of +30 / -30. And the matrix also shows potential for conflict: because each of the projects can have a negative impact on some objectives. How realistic!

Integration of existing projects

These seven points constitute the one task which we were supposed to work on in the coming weeks. And all that on top of our daily operational time!

However, there was yet another job in addition to that. This was the task of listing all ongoing as well as planned projects as previously agreed upon with our financial director.

The list should contain the following:

- The approved project expenditure,
- The proportion so far used, and
- The persons involved.

We wanted to discuss these aspects in seven weeks' time. The intention was to examine whether the ongoing projects fitted into our strategic house and how we wanted to proceed from there.

Our decision-making workshop

We met again in a similar session after seven weeks. I actually thought that I had our company "under control" - but I fear I have again had to learn something new!

Concentrating on essential projects

When the already ongoing projects were introduced, certain things came up which I partly didn't know anymore, and partly didn't know yet, but also those that I thought were already accomplished long ago. It was only when the individual projects were discussed, that we then understood what we had achieved seven weeks ago: a structured collection of strategic issues really perceived by all of us to be important.

However, it was now going to be actually quite easy for us to cancel all ongoing but not yet concluded old projects- except for...., well, that was of course the problem:

Example:
>In the case of the project titled "Catering for old people", a kind of lunch table on wheels, we had already spent 170 T€. That had not featured in our brainstorming.
>Forgotten? Not productive? Unimportant?

Thanks to our strategic house, we realised that this project would actually not fit into our planned structure any more.

In that situation the good business lady knows only one thing: stop and try to silver-coat the incurred expenses as much as possible. It doesn't help really to immediately decide to spend another 30 k€ only to realise: "what do we do with this now?"

In that way, a project like this one, started or not yet started, became a victim of our earlier strategic assessments. Since none of us was left unscathed, we were able to negotiate with each other without many personal problems. Of course we became unfaithful to ourselves two or three times, but there must be exceptions in life!

And we are able to turn over four old projects to the project teams with a clean conscience, since they matched our strategic coordinates.

Jochen Bierath, our financial director, was happy that we had managed to save 450 k€ on our own for the coming year.

Deciding on strategic projects

We could really use the money, and also the time which had become free well enough, because the presentation of the new projects was coming next. Each of us presented the results of the group work, outlined the expenditure and strategic returns of the projects, and tried to convince the others that his project should of course be implemented as quickly as possible according to the project plans.

Jochen was however not all together satisfied; 1,300 k€ were required of him in the coming year - a bit too much! Even the 450 k€ saved through our write-off action could not prevent him from exercising his power of veto. We therefore had to struggle among ourselves for project budgets.

Even though policy-makers always try to fool us now and again, the lawn-mower method is probably the most unsuitable way to cut costs. One can of course simply vote in the executive board to decide which project or which strategic projects should be postponed or even be written off completely. With the integration of the projects into the strategic coordinates, there is nevertheless a possibility for us to weight the projects, and that weighting does not have absolute significance but rather a relative one.

The outcome of our discussions, supported by the respective project weightings, was that we decided to immediately implement the following four projects:

Project	Planned expenditure in the first year
Project 1: Engagement for senior citizens	270 k€
Project 2: Structural adjustment	165 k€
Project 3: Further training	420 k€
Project 6: Partner region	95 k€
Planned expenditure in the first year:	950 k€

Project management of the strategic projects

Afterwards we decided on the people who were going to be responsible as project managers for these four strategic projects. They were not in all cases the temporary project managers selected in the first hour. But the latter were supposed to at least monitor the project as "patrons" and to ensure that they are carried out successfully. And they were also to fight for "their" project, to support the project manager if it came to fights over allocations - as it always happens under a matrix structure.

We wanted to make a review in six month´s time and decide whether to start the remaining three projects or probably to revise them in a new BSC-round.

Was that the end?
The work then started in earnest! We determined the ACTUAL values for our target ratios (key objective, strategic topics and development areas) and we set the planned values (whereupon yet more discussions ensued because this was now about something concrete).

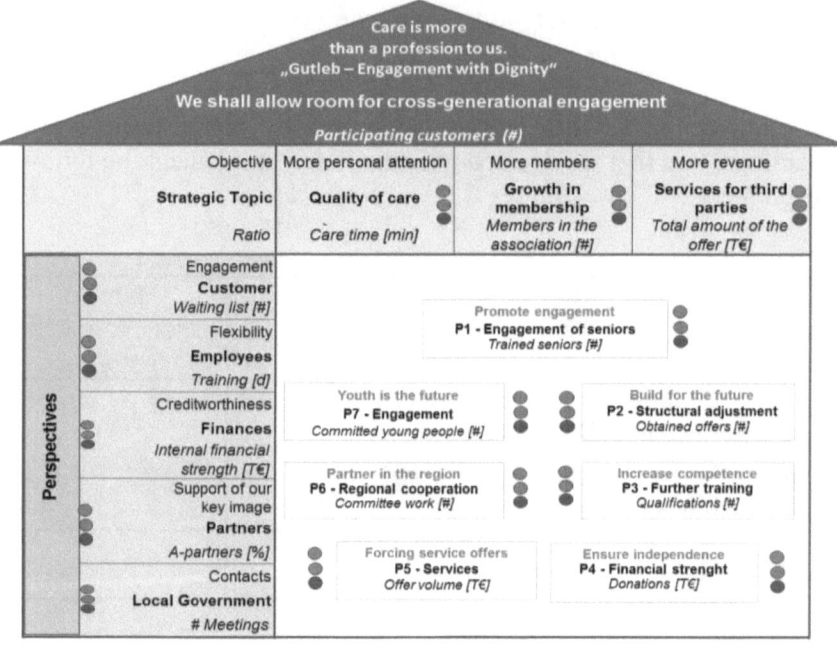

Our strategic house (Management-Scorecard)

Every quarter we would meet in our strategic round and we also looked at the strategic numbers - we called that tableau the "Management Balanced Scorecard", for it always led us back to reality with its lights, and it showed us where the problem was.

We let ourselves be encouraged by our Balanced Scorecard to take care of strategic issues on top of our operational activities. But had we not been doing that already before? Yes of course, but everyone was doing his own thing. However, we are now working in a process with one target - each one with his own responsibility for strategic projects that are jointly worked out and agreed upon; projects which are all directed at a common goal:

Care is more than just a profession to us

„Gutleb – Engagement with Dignity"

2.7 Step 5: Our Reporting Scorecard

Using the Reporting Scorecard, we lay out the most important goals for the operational and strategic business clearly on a sheet of paper:

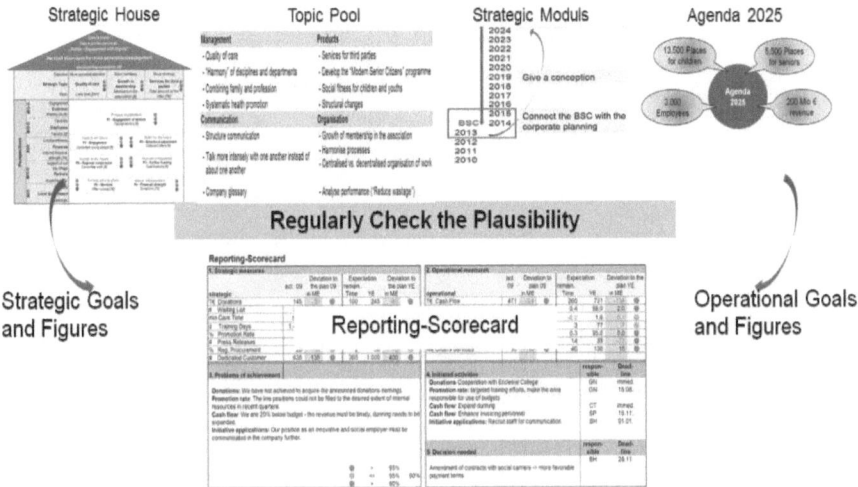

Sources of the Reporting Scorecard

We worked out the first approach for this in a small group. We did that with ratios which we use to document the implementation of the strategy and the use of potentials created in the process.

The Reporting Scorecard has above all an internal control-function for us: Do we ensure that the targeted operational goals (cash flow, utilization, incoming orders for the services sector etc.) are also safeguarded through strategic measures and projects? And: What effects can we expect from our strategic projects (care, employee commitment, further training, and press work) in operational results?

However, we should also inform third parties, our principle banks, the regional public as well as other interested third parties about our strategic and operational work. One can use the Reporting Scorecard form for that purpose too.

What appears important to me in that process is that we should always think of the recipient of the report; what type of information should the recipient get or does the recipient want to get concerning our strategy implementation and utilisation of potentials?

> **Example:**
> A BSC-reporting structure is mandatory in large enterprises as well as in agencies with many hierarchy levels. This leads, for instance, to such meaningful ratios as the "punctuality ratio" for railways management (!) in the case of the Railways-Strategy-Card of the Deutsche Bahn.
> Other enterprises like the Heidelberger Druck AG, for instance, divide the Balanced Scorecard into two thirds for the reporting part and one third for personal information.

We have put the focus of our Reporting Scorecard on the "target-achievement-forecast". That's why when it comes to content, the issue is particularly about the measures and decisions which have to be introduced in order to realise those goals.

We regularly report internally to the group of participants in our strategy workshop. At the same time all the management executives discuss the information with their own teams.

Do good and talk about it !

Externally we want to talk to our principle banks and also to our key regional partners about our strategic work. By doing that, we achieve one thing – as a side-effect so to say - namely that our Balanced Scorecard receives stronger commitment through regular reports.

Reporting Scorecard (09/2016)

1. Strategic measures

strategic	Act. 09	Deviation to the Plan 09 in ME		Expectation remain. Time	YE	Deviation to the Plan YE in ME	
k€ Donations	145	-30	●	100	245	-80	●
# Waiting list	300	0	●	-20	280	0	●
min Care time	14,5	-0	●	0,5	15,0	-1	○
d Training days	1.400	0	●	630	2.030	230	●
% Promotion rate	33	-5	●	1	34	-4	●
# Press releases	30	8	●	12	42	7	●
% Reg. procurement	28	-2	○	2	30	-3	○
# Dedicated customer	635	135	●	365	1.000	400	●

3. Problems of achievement

Donations: We have not achieved to acquire the announced donations earnings.
Promotion rate: The line positions could not be filled to the desired extent of internal resources in recent quarters.
Cash flow: We are 20% below budget - the revenue must be timely, dunning needs to be expanded.
Initiative applications: Our position as an innovative and social employer must be communicated in the company further.

●	>	95%
◐	<>	95% 90%
●	>	90%

Our Reporting Scorecard (left-hand side)

2. Operational measures

operational	Act. 09	Deviation to Plan 09 in ME		Expectation remain. Time	YE	Deviation to the Plan YE in ME	
k€ Cash flow	471	-94	●	260	731	-134	●
% Utilisation rate	97,6	1,1	●	0,4	98,0	2,0	●
Customer satisfaction	1,8	0,1	●	-0,2	1,6	-0,1	○
% Level of competence	74	-8	○	3	77	-7	○
% Attendance rate	94,7	-1,3	●	0,3	95,0	0,0	●
# Initiative applications	25	-7	●	14	39	-13	●
M€ Orders services	90	15	●	40	130	15	●

4. Initiated activities	respon-sible	Dead-line
Donations Cooperation with Ecclesial College	GN	immed.
Promotion rate: targeted training efforts, make the area responsible for use of budgets	GN	15.08.
Cash flow: Expend dunning	CT	immed.
Cash flow: Enhance invoicing personnel	SP	15.11.
Initiative applications: Recruit staff for communication	BH	01.01.

5. Decision needed	respon-sible	Dead-line
	BH	28.11.
Amendment of contracts with social carriers -> more favorable payment terms		

Our Reporting Scorecard (right-hand side)

We dress our information for third parties outside the company, for instance during presentations, with the following story:

Gutleb – Engagement with Dignity

We consistently ensure that our employees receive further training and the outcome of this is that we can fill the majority of our management positions with people taken from among our own staff. This is an important factor in motivating our employees, which translates into committed, error-free work and a high rate of attendance.

True to our slogan, "Engagement with Dignity", we attach importance to active and committed participation of the customer base in our institutions and hence give the senior citizens and children/youths alike dignity by granting them the opportunity to participate in our work. Through those efforts we achieve an outstanding degree of customer satisfaction and positive feedback from the media.

Another key criterion for good care is the supply of fresh products from the home region.

As a result of these efforts and the activities of our organisation, we are able to realize a high demand for our capacities and to register a high level of occupancy. That leads to a payment surplus (cash flow), which for our business sector is gratifying, and which we shall use for further expansion of our social institutions.

Wouldn't you too invest in this company? Wouldn't you support the Gutleb Organisation in realising their social goals? Our story is correct, because we shall do something for the future of the "stakeholders" of Gutleb-Association, for our employees, our partners, our customers, and our financiers. And we safeguard the future of our region.

The Balanced Scorecard as a basis for a comprehensive strategic reporting system

Even with this Reporting Scorecard we do not yet have a comprehensive strategic reporting system. It is a first approach. To begin with, we shall use the ratios contained in it as a basis for the annual planning and budgeting process. From there we shall promise ourselves a closer linkage between the strategic and operational actions.

At the same time we shall look for ways of designing our budgeting process in a more flexible manner and developing our employees' personal initiative further. It is a long journey but for sure I will be able to follow the business discussions as a pensioner.

2.8 Step 6: Integrating in the management process

Our management team meets every month to discuss the results of the period just ended and to derive decisions from it for operational action. That leads to a higher degree of flexibility and is certainly the reason for our economic success. Another reason is that for us, the budget is not a rule which must be obeyed at all costs. Our budget leaves room for manoeuvre and gives those responsible for the various institutions freedom to react to new situations in a flexible manner – they are responsible for the end result and not just for the budget.

We also decided during those meetings to pursue the implementation of our strategic objectives using the strategic house and the reporting scorecard. It is important to note that for every ratio there is a person responsible. This creates commitment.

Through that exercise we managed to set in motion a continuous learning process. On the one hand we check whether we are doing something for the future of our company as agreed upon. On the other hand we ask ourselves whether strategic and operational management are still "on course", whether we are still moving in the right direction or whether we have to correct ourselves.

We had decided during the decision-making workshop to introduce the Balanced Scorecard management method to administrative staff as well, both at the youth care centre and the old people's home – on a trial basis. However we did not want to simulate the strategic projects. The heads of those departments – and, by the way, also an external "friend of the house" – should draft their own scorecards. The respective head of department (who participated in our workshop) has explained the key objective. True, the strategic topics as well as the development areas of the institutions differed from each other, but they supported our key objective.

Even managers of the multidisciplinary strategic projects took part in those workshops (of course only managers of projects involved in that particular sector!). Their participation was, on the one hand, to collect good ideas from participants of those multidisciplinary projects, on the other hand, to avoid duplication of their own projects.

Incidentally, these sector-workshops lasted only one to two days. There was no need to once again carry out strategy discussions so intensively – and the strategic projects were designed in a less elaborate manner.

2.9 Step 7: Learning from experience

Just after half a year I started getting this rumbling feeling: The project management for our Project 2 - "Building for the Future" – had whirled a lot; they had improved jointly thought-out ideas and had done a lot for their implementation. But the result was not any better, judging by the number of offers received.

When we saw nothing happening even by the end of the next quarter, we decided to stop the project for the time being.

Hold annual strategy-workshops.
In that way you will be able to
- Make an assessment of what has been achieved so far,
- Re-examine the strategic coordinate system and probably even
* the key objective and key image and*
- Collect and implement ideas for new actions.

The strategy workshop which took place after one year, and which involved fresh collection of ideas for targeted actions, gave us the opportunity to set new milestones.

This was also logical: For one thing, our Project 6 – "Regional Co-operation" - was very successful, such that we were able to turn our strategic attention to other issues and regional co-operation became part of our day-to-day operations. Potentials created in the project are now being used to our advantage.

We laid a new focus for Project 2 – "Building for the Future" – on the improvement of internal business processes which were meant to offer committed senior citizens and adolescents the opportunity to get involved. We also selected a new ratio for Project 2: "The number of engagement-oriented business processes".

And so the Strategy-Implementation-Workshops (we could never really come to terms with the abbreviation BSC) have slowly become part of our annual planning calendar, and the Balanced Scorecard Management Method has become part of our daily life.

3 Implementation of the BSC in a Company

How do we organise the consistent introduction and propagation of a Balanced Scorecard in the company? Which tasks can a software program undertake in that process? Should one combine selected ratios with premiums?

There is no one correct way, just as there is no right Balanced Scorecard. There is only a suitable path to a Balanced Scorecard customised to the needs of our company. And there are empirical values which one can take into consideration along the way.

One precondition for the joint drawing up of a Balanced Scorecard is readiness to engage in open dialogue. We must learn to take our colleagues as partners and to bring them along the shared path of making the Balanced Scorecard. Management by "instruction and mistrust (control)" might still be practised in some companies, but in modern society we increasingly need people who think along, act along and are co-responsible in order to succeed amidst all the competition. For that we also need to act independently and to make independent decisions, as well as being open and honest.

Companies which until now were being managed in a hierarchical setup are likely to need a longer period of time to build up trust. We at the Gutleb-Association have been trying for years now to practise openness to our employees. And we are increasingly getting back exactly what we gave: independent and responsible action!

Was it actually difficult to organise our workshop for drafting the Balanced Scorecard? No, not really. We were supported by Klaus Marwitz and the moderators recommended by him. But allow me to enumerate the most important points that can get a company fit for the BSC:

3.1 How to begin? Always from top to bottom?

Actually the motto "from top to bottom" applies. Nevertheless we have been wondering whether we should not first begin with the scorecard in one sector. This path is also feasible so long as the boss takes part in the sector-workshop and supports or at least tolerates matters arising from it. Besides, it would be good if there was a strategic target orientation of the whole company, so that one does not have to start from the beginning again later on. We thought we had this – at least before we held our workshop.

Our moderators talked about the sub-sectors of other companies, which had attained good success as "side-entrants" with the introduction of their Balanced Scorecard – and possessed more freedoms for the implementation of strategic objectives than they believed to be having.

In our BSC-workshop we designed the strategic house as well as the reporting-scorecard for the entire organisation, that is to say, for our company. We shall later pass on the results to the various sectors, so that they can develop their own scorecards.

3.2   Who should take part in a BSC-workshop?

All management staff of the company or of the department for which a Balanced Scorecard is supposed to be developed should be involved. That's what we pushed through. Nobody was supposed to disengage himself from the exercise and later torpedo the process. Luckily enough we don't have 24 directors like some other big companies.

Due to group dynamics, such a workshop was not supposed to be held with more than 15 people. As a reminder: in our case the people who took part are the four members of the top-most managerial level (commercial management, personnel management, purchase/ organisation, and myself as the chief executive officer) , two managers a piece for our institutions (elderly and the youth), our workers´ council chairperson and Mr. Marwitz from the association's board of directors. In addition, one representative of the parents and one member of the residential homes´ council also attended.

In order to absorb new ideas and thoughts, we also requested three young colleagues to join in the workshop, with the hope that they will become part of our management team in a few years´ time - open-minded thinkers, so to speak.

I didn't actually want our female employees' representative to be on that team - she seemed to me to be too circumspect. However our moderators insisted on it. And lo and behold, she has performed so superbly well that it later became easier to convince all employees to accept the objectives.

The workers´ council representative should always be part of the BSC-team. The strategic objectives proposed here mostly have co-determination effects. And now you have the workers´ council representative on board, because it is actually his ideas that are currently supposed to be implemented!

3.3   When and where?

The best time for a BSC-workshop is in spring or early summer. This is not just because we feel the vigour of sprouting nature in us during those months, but more especially because the Balanced Scorecard can best be incorporated into the annual business calendar at that time: March/April for drafting/clarifying the strategy, May or June for drawing up the objectives and projects of the strategic house, then seven weeks for designing the project, and finally the resolution during the decision-making workshop and the drawing up of the reporting scorecard. The approved costs for the strategic projects can then be absorbed into the medium-term plan and budget for the coming year.

But even if the BSC-process is initiated at any other time of the year: the medium-term plan and budget should be handled in such a flexible manner that projects can be started even at that time, if they are decided upon not before February, for instance, and are not found in the current planning documents.

The BSC-workshop should as much as possible not be held at the company premises. Interruptions occasioned by telephone calls, or having to go and sign a document, etc. are not suitable for such a process which is driven by group dynamics. Therefore, a (not so nearby) hotel for instance, with sufficient room for group sessions and a stimulating atmosphere, which also offers room for evening interaction, is preferable.

3.4   Who will do the moderation?

A prophet is never accepted in his own country - this saying applies to us too. We have some colleagues in the Gutleb-Association who can moderate such a workshop well. However, they are not neutral - they have their own interests i.e. they always take sides in the BSC - process, whether they like it or not. When we are affected, we cannot stand by and let things happen. That's why one should work together with external moderators.

This applies at least to the top most management level! For the introduction of the BSC into our institutions, we trained 2 internal BSC moderators who will monitor and moderate the process further - but not in their own sectors!

3.5 Keeping the process running

Strategy development and implementation is the top most management task. **And we have to stick to it!** Everyone has probably had this experience before. Every now and then things don't work out smoothly in the company. Then fire-fighting measures have to be instituted, in order to straighten things out again or to prevent worse things from happening. If business operations are not running, then strategic tasks will remain unattended to and at a stand-still.

The implementation of a strategy at the Gutleb-Association therefore rests with me as the managing director. My assistant who is the officer in charge of BSC affairs is responsible for seeing to it that we take ourselves seriously. His task is to continuously bother us until it becomes second nature to us. We must always do something for our future even in our daily work!

3.6 Strategic ratios as a measure for premiums?

The Gutleb-Association maintains close cooperation between management and the workers´ council. In that connection, we found opportunities of stimulating the assumption of responsibility even with premiums. I know this discussion and I believe I am aware of the advantages and disadvantages of premiums.

We should at this point differentiate between two groups of recipients:

- Employees whose pay is just enough for their daily subsistence,
- Management staff and experts for whom it is more important to have fun at work and to be accorded recognition.

Bill Gates once said that it is difficult to lure millionaires into working more innovatively using premiums (30% of the Microsoft employees are said to be millionaires). I had the same experience. It is true, my management team are not millionaires, but some of them could earn more money elsewhere. They choose to remain with us because we have fast decision making structures and flat hierarchies, and because we offer them the chance to take over responsibility. And what could be more motivating than the opportunity to shape things?

We of course get our management staff to also be involved in the end result, but that does not have a big enough effect on motivation in my view. Nevertheless we have undertaken, after one year's experience with the Balanced Scorecard, to also include the strategic attainment of objectives in the calculation of premiums.

Our "normal" employees do their best day after day so as to earn their daily bread. But they too want to propel Gutleb into further development. We know that from our customers whose experience from immediate contact with those employees is largely positive. In that case we can only convey our appreciation to those workers with premiums. Money has a different kind of weight for people who earn less.

We have learnt that workers like educators, nurses for elderly people or cleaning ladies love assuming responsibility - responsibility for the respective department where they work - and they also love being independent within the framework of their job.

Example:
This is how a project team in one of our old people's institutions, which is already working with the Balanced Scorecard, got down to work in support of autonomy. Even the ladies in charge of cleaning in this institution have been given their own areas of responsibility and a budget allocation for cleaning materials which they manage independently and for which they only account once every three months

---

It works. Of course there are clashes sometimes, but there is a growing sense of understanding for each other in our organisation, because everybody is looking at him-/herself more and more as an entrepreneur within his/her department. Being demanding and supportive at the same time - this works even internally!

3.7 Software support

We hesitated for a long time: Should we use a software solution to facilitate the process of drawing up the BSC in the company? There are many offers for such programs. The costs for the software, and especially for their introduction, are not quite without their own problems! After we had carried out the first discussions about introducing the Balanced Scorecard, it became clear to us: this is about management and not ostensibly about ratios. Therefore it is also not important to start with a software solution right at the outset. A spreadsheet program like MS Excel has been absolutely sufficient for us in the presentation of ratios. What appeared to be more important to us is the inclusion of the expected expenses and results into the medium-term plan.

ratios cost money!

We now "live" with the Balanced Scorecard and have gotten used to measuring the results of strategic actions. And we draw consequences from it.

Each manager of a strategic project receives a printout every month containing the costs and time spent, as well as investments. They are collected and processed with the help of our commercial software and then transferred to Excel.

What about the "strategic earnings", where will they come from? We have considered specific ratios for our actions (OAR) numbering to well over 100. For the strategic coordinates specifically should we measure all of them? "No", our BSC-moderators elaborated. "We should never forget: Even the processing of ratios costs time and money".

> **Example**:
>   Is it worth recording a ratio for a project step lasting perhaps three
>   months with project costs amounting to 12 k€?

Therefore they recommended that we should concentrate on a few ratios which are effective for maintaining the BSC-process. Does the volume of information and leadership skill justify the time and money spent on determining and processing the data underlying the ratios?

To them, one principle was of utmost importance: ratios are supposed to steer us into the future. But if we get up-to-date values only once a year, then it becomes difficult to carry out such a task as steering. That's why all selected parameters must be recorded at least every quarter.

We have left it to the respective project managers to decide on their own which ratios they want to record. For that purpose, a target figure of not more than 3 % of the total cost was set.

On the other hand we wanted at any rate to capture the ratios for strategic projects, strategic coordinates and our key objective and to evaluate them every quarter in the guidance and reporting scorecards.

Where shall we get this information from? For every ratio we set the source of information and the department responsible/ in charge:

The strategic ratios of Gutleb-Association

Objective	Ratio	Available?	Period	Data source/ in-charge
Key objective	Number of customers involved	No	monthly	Monthly statistics for institutions
Strategic topic 1: Quality of care	Time used for care	partly	monthly	Time-recording system, even for volunteers
Strategic topic 2: Growth in membership	Number of organisation's members	Yes	monthly	Organisation's statistics
Strategic topic 3: Services for 3rd parties	Total number of orders	No	monthly	Statistics of offers
Perspective: Customers	Number of persons on our waiting list	No	quarterly	Public relations
Perspective: Employees	Number of training days	Yes	quarterly	Personnel department
Perspective: Finances	Internal financial strength (cash flow/balance sheet total)	Yes	quarterly	Accounting
Perspective: Local Government	Number of A-partners	No	quarterly	Purchase

Objective	Ratio	Available?	Period	Data source/ in-charge
Local politics Development area	Number of meetings with regionally important personalities	No	quarterly	Public relations
Project 1: Engagement for senior citizens	Number of trained senior citizens	No	monthly	Monthly statistics for institutions
Project 2: Structural adjustment	Number of orders received	No	quarterly	Purchase
Project 3: Further training	Qualifications attained	No	quarterly	Personnel department
Project 4: Financial strength *	Donations	Yes	monthly	Organisation's statistics
Project 5: Services*	Total number of orders	Yes	quarterly	Accounting
Project 6: Partner Region	Number of committee participations	No	quarterly	Public relations
Project 7: Engagement for youths*	Number of children/youths involved	No	monthly	Time-recording system, even for volunteers

* Project will be pursued later

Strategic ratios

Strategic management with measurable objectives is closely linked with operational management through the strategic house and the reporting scorecard, as well as their integration into the medium-term plan, and has found its permanent place in our management calendar.

3.8 Building consequence management

We have nevertheless had to learn that all those measures are not enough. Consequence does not grow from numbers - it is a management task:

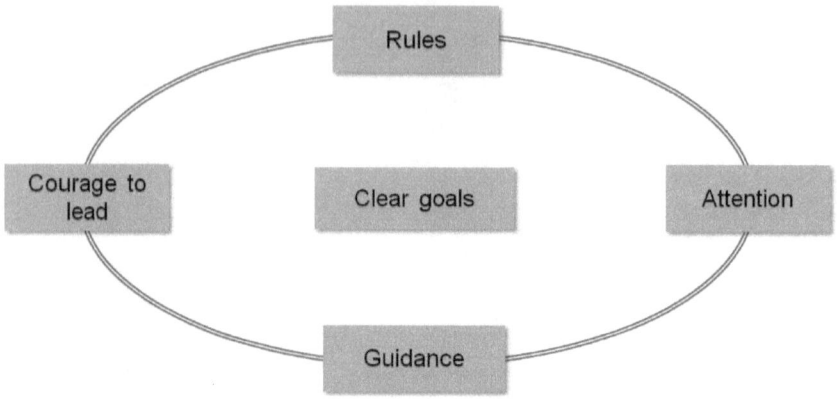

Elements of consequence management

There had been a lot to do:

- We had given ourselves clear goals.
- We didn't have defined rules for managerial work. We don't want to exaggerate that either. But two or three simple principles can still be of help. We introduced a new rule:
  For coming late or for the ringing of a cell-phone during meetings, one pays € 5. The proceeds will be spent on social causes. This measure contributed more to discipline than I had ever anticipated.
  We are currently trying out a second rule:
  Each manager takes the area of competence which he needs and expresses readiness to suffer a "bloody nose" for it from time to time. That could spur his autonomy on. Let's see where that will lead us.
- Attention is probably the "Alpha" and "Omega" of each consequence. People read what is and what is not important to us from our attention. After telling my trainee probably 20 times that in our organisation people greet each other when they meet, he has come to know, that greeting is important to me - and he has done it ever since! That's why we are focussing on a "handful" of objectives. We cannot afford to direct our attention to more than those.

- The guidance using the Strategic House (Management Scorecard and the Reporting Scorecard is running quite well.
- What is remaining is courage to lead: Decision-making, removal of obstacles from employees´paths, allowing them to act on their own and taking care of themselves.

Are we more successful with the Balanced Scorecard?

We have co-existed with our Balanced Scorecard for some time now. Has it brought us any progress?

It is not so easy to answer this question with "yes" or "no". We have made the following observation - you can draw your own conclusion from it:

- Our management staff workshop on the Balanced Scorecard had brought unbelievable amounts of motivation.

  Many issues had finally been expressed. It was liberating to have a jointly-developed and shared strategy, and to have understood, what each person can do for that strategy. The same effect was also registered during the subsequent workshops in our reference institutions.

- Since all BSC-workshops end with clear work instructions, this mood had to be kept up. Implementation means work - and it quickly became clear to us that we need time, resources and consequence for this.

  The "write-off concept" in our "old" projects at the decision-making workshop brought frustration to some of us. However, we forced ourselves to concentrate our efforts on what was really important. And since we had agreed together on a few new strategic projects, everybody was relieved in the end. We saved time and resources!

- The wind of change has not yet set in some institutions. In particular we have not been successful everywhere in removing fears from those who have not yet been integrated into the Balanced Scorecard; fears of change, fears of new developments.

- Our task in that regard is to communicate the common goals to everybody in a more understandable manner. I in particular, as chief executive, made that my goal. I will try to get myself involved in as many strategy-workshops as possible. Isn't safeguarding the future the top-most responsibility of a chief executive?

- Our partners, suppliers, local authorities and banks are impressed! We promise security and the capability of being a reliable partner. And that is increasingly being felt and seen through our actions.

- Gratifyingly, we keep hearing from more and more institutions "When can we develop our own Balanced Scorecard?"

  Particularly those at management level are realising that the method of management which involves the Balanced Scorecard simplifies leadership, enables the passing on of responsibility to others, and supports the most important task in a company - safeguarding the future.

- Our business performance has not improved in the last two years. How come? We have invested a lot in people, both employees and customers, and in processes. This costs money which our accounting department records as expenditure, although it is actually investment in our future. The mere fact that our performance has not worsened either, speaks for itself!

- The most beautiful side of it, though, is that the young and the old feel better cared for in our institutions. They are not only cared for, but also treated as partners; supported and tasked with responsibility at the same time. That gives them energy, and in the case of our senior citizens in particular it makes them feel wanted / needed again.

From practical experience, we are able to look to the future with more confidence today than was the case two years ago. And even if I am soon going to step down from the management of Gutleb-Association, I know that my colleagues are well prepared.

Our future has become more secure through this. We feel that we are on the right track, even if the way ahead is still going to be arduous and full of work.

Thanks to our Balanced Scorecard, the Gutleb- Association can safely say:

Welcome to the Future!

4 Checklist for the Balanced Scorecard

You will find the most important points for the development and implementation of a Balanced Scorecard in the following check-list.

But remember: There is no royal path when it comes to the Balanced Scorecard, no single correct way - just as there is also no "correct" Balanced Scorecard. Your Balanced Scorecard must be tailored to the needs of your company.

Firstly, as a basis: strategic target setting	✓

This is where you determine the run-up period, and analyse the state of the company and the strategic objective. Important: Exchange ideas with each other because this is the basis for common action!

- Analyse the current situation:
    - Maintain the "creative tension" between reality and strategic objectives: Where do we stand, and where do we want to go?
    - Don't work with too much paper: What you don't have in you "head and stomach", is of no use to you!
- Talk about common basic values. Values are the stabilising element, the "anchor" in the storm of changes.
- Discuss and agree on the business idea for your company
    - Values and identity: Why are we proud to work here?
    - Vision: What do we strive for?
    - Mission: For whom are we there?
    - Why are you a company?
    - Why don't you earn your money as a "chips- stand"?
- Explain the business idea through a business model.
    - What makes you unique?
    - Which needs do your customers have?
    - How do those customers "tick"?
    - With which core competencies can you serve the needs of your customers better than your competitors?
- Concretise the business idea through a core benefit (product, a good, price, permitted costs)
- Integrate the personal objectives of those involved, then your future dreams will by far have a greater chance of being realised.
- Set an agenda as a guide for the size of operational business you are striving for in x years.
- Explain the agenda through a projection of the most important indicators and determine the appropriate strategic milestones.
- Develop a store of topics for the most important tasks of product development, management, organisation and communication.

1 What needs to be done now: Key objective and key image   ✓
- Concretise the time frame "now".
- Develop the key image from the mission:
  - How does the company want to be viewed in the coming years?
  - Who do you want to be?
  - What do you offer (against what does your client measure his success in relation to your performance)?
  - How do you portray yourself?
  - How do you get to the "back of your customer's mind"?
- Try to find a catchy slogan which conveys your key image - this is seldom possible with the first throw of the dice!
- Derive a key objective:
  - What does the company want to have achieved in the next few years?
  - What is necessary for you to maintain your market position (minimum)?
  - What do you consider to be worth striving for (standard)?
  - What is possible (maximum)?
  - What decisions must you make today, and which ones can you make later?
  - Which decisions should you prepare?
  - Which eventualities must you prepare yourself for?
- Determine the indicator for the key objective: Use that key indicator to create awareness of the key objective for everybody in the company!

2 Strategic coordinate system in the strategic house   ✓
- Derive the strategic topics for the attainment of the key objective; also use the topic pool for this purpose:
  - As much as possible choose not more than four, better less, topics and focus your strategic actions on them.
  - What are the crucial areas of emphasis?
- Choose an indicator for each strategic topic. That will help you to concretise the objective. (What do you want to measure yourself against?)
- Delimit the development areas (perspectives), with which the expectations of the key stakeholders can be described in your company:
  - Find your perspectives, define your key stakeholders – each company is different!
  - Try to concentrate on the sub-sectors of the development areas! – Less is more!
- Determine an indicator for each development area respectively (Perspectives). With that indicator, you will be able to concretise the interests of your respective stakeholders.

3 Actions in the strategic coordinate system   ✓

Your strategic topics (columns) and the development areas (rows) form the "inner matrix" of your strategic house. Through that you get development fields which you then fill with ideas for actions.

- Collect concrete ideas in a structured manner for the implementation of strategies (OAR):
    - Collect 80 to 150 ideas in the company for targeted actions taking into consideration the previously determined strategic coordinates.
    - For each action, define:
    ° **Objective** of the action
    ° **Action** content (as concrete as possible)
    ° **Ratio**, against which you want to measure the process (early indicator) or the result (late indicator) of the action.
    Stick to OAR!
    - Examine and justify the interaction between the objectives of your actions and those of the respective development areas, and also those of the strategic topics.

4 Bundling actions to strategic projects and implementing those projects   ✓

- Group your actions:
    - Group them together according to related contents (across all strategic topics and development areas).
    - Be mindful of the problems relating to responsibilities and jurisdictions.
    - Form project ideas from the clusters.
- Determine an indication for each project idea. You will then concretise the objective of your projects with that ratio.
(What do you want to measure yourself against?)
- Review the project ideas:
    1 Form a small working group, a team of three to maximum five employees, who will structure the strategic project ideas.
        - The respective team leaders should be selected from the circle of those who worked on the management-BSC; although it is not a must, they can nevertheless be identical with the leaders who would later head the project.
    2 Set the project objective.
    3 Define the project indicator, the actual and target values as well as milestones for the project indicator.
    4 Fill in the missing actions/ partial project steps to the project structure.
    5 Set the chronological order of the project steps.
    6 Work out the necessary resources (investments, costs, time).
    7 Try to determine the impact of the strategic project on the company objective, the matrix composed of strategic topics and development areas.
- Adopt the strategic projects within the context of the decision-making workshop.
    - The project leaders will talk about their strategic projects in about 7 weeks' time.
    - The management team discusses and selects the strategic projects (preferably not all), and they propose the future budgets for the next period(s).

- Examine all ongoing projects:
  - Which other projects are in the "pipeline" and can be cancelled, because they do not comply with the strategic objectives drawn up?
  - Open up scope for your strategic BSC-projects in that way.
  - Be honest with yourself! However: One can sometimes also afford "luxuries" for oneself!
- Specify the persons in charge of the projects. Take some time for your future, and get involved in working in strategic projects.
- Determine a person authorised to take care of BSC affairs and a project sponsor. Who will responsibly take care of the implementation of future tasks? Most preferably the company management!

5 Managing and reporting with the Balanced Scorecard

- Determine the target committees/persons for reporting purposes.
  - Who should receive the reporting scorecard, and how often?
  - What should the internal recipients know, and what the external recipients?
- Derive suitable ratios for the reporting scorecard. In doing so, pay attention to the structures of the strategic house selected by you, and your agenda for operational business.
  - Try to find some indicators, with whose help you can best tell third parties the "story" of how you will implement your strategies. The said third parties don't necessarily have to know the details, but they should be able to understand, accept and endorse the story.
  - Bear in mind the costs of the indicators!
- Use the strategic house as internal management scorecard.

6 Merging of the BSC into the management process

- Specify the business sectors, which are earmarked for the development of their own Balanced Scorecard.
  - Which business sectors are strategically relevant?
  - Where are different strategic approaches for the attainment of the key objective meaningful and necessary?

Caution:
The key objective of the company is binding for everybody – the strategic topics on the other hand are no longer considered to be so.

- Connect the ratio with responsibility.

7 Utilising feedback and learning processes

- Go over the performance results of the strategic projects once every three months. The strategic house is the "Future-Gutleb Org" of your company and it signals the need for action:
  - Examine project progress,
  - Bear in mind the effects of the project,
  - Possibly match project structures with the changed conditions,
  - Rethink all your strategies and show readiness to correct false assumptions.
- Revise your Balanced Scorecard annually, if possible every six months.
  - Are the basic assumptions, the key objective and the strategic coordinates still correct?
  - Must strategic projects be revised, new projects started?
  - Is the budget framework sufficient?
  - Fit projects into the budget of the coming year.
  - Can we steer the company effectively using the objectives and ratios of the reporting scorecard?
- Build an effective consequence management system!

Recommended Internet / Literature References

Recommended web sites

www.scorecard.de
This is the German language website for the dissemination of information on the Balanced Scorecard, as well as showing the current state of research and practice relate to it. You will find, among other things, a detailed up-to-date list of literature references and practice-related reports there. Provider: Friedag Consult and ask Dr. Schmidt, both from Berlin

www.thepalladiumgroup.com
The US-Consultancy Agency Palladium run by Robert Kaplan and David P. Norton is behind the "Palladium Group".

Recommended Literature

There have been many books and essays on the Balanced Scorecard published in the German-speaking region in the last few years. Most of them pertain to the strategic reporting system known as the "Balanced Scorecard". This corresponds roughly to the approach put forward by Kaplan/Norton in 1992.

The authors of this pocket guide began to describe in 1999 a truly practice-oriented method and they have continued to expand that approach. Kaplan/Norton also followed that path, and they talk about it, among other things, in their book: "The Strategy-Focused Organization".

The following English or German publications give a picture of the current approaches on the topic of the Balanced Scorecard:

Abel, Roland/Wannöffel, Dr. Manfred: Die Balanced Scorecard als Bestandteil der Betriebsratsarbeit, Düsseldorf 2002

Drucker, Peter: On the Profession of Management, Boston 2003

Ehrmann, Harald: Kompakttraining Balanced Scorecard, Ludwigshafen 2007

Friedag, Herwig R./Schmidt, Walter: My Balanced Scorecard, 3. Auflage, Freiburg 2006

Friedag, Herwig R./Schmidt, Walter: Management 2.0: Kooperation – Der entscheidende Wettbewerbsvorteil, Freiburg 2009

Friedag, Herwig R./Schmidt, Walter: Balanced Scorecard – einfach konsequent, Freiburg 2014

Gälweiler, Aloys: Strategische Unternehmensführung, 3. Auflage, Frankfurt/Main 2005

Horváth & Partner: Balanced Scorecard umsetzen, Stuttgart 2007

Kaplan, Robert S./Norton, David P.: The Strategy-Focused Organization: How Balanced Scorecard Companies Thrive in the New Business Environment, Boston 2000

Kaplan, Robert S./Norton, David P.: The Balanced Scorecard: Translating Strategy into Action, Boston 1996

Weber, Jürgen/Schäffer, Utz: Balanced Scorecard und Controlling, Wiesbaden 2000

Glossary of keywords   English – German (a)

agenda	Agenda	43
bonus	Prämie	82
business model	Geschäftsmodell	42
checklist Balanced Scorecard	Checkliste Balanced Scorecard	88
coherence	Stimmigkeit	20
common objectives	gemeinsame Ziele	21
consequence	Konsequenz	86
core expertise	Leistungskern	40
critical success factor	kritischer Erfolgsfaktor	11
decision workshop	Entscheidungsworkshop	69
development areas	Entwicklungsgebiete	11
early and late ratio	Früh- und Spätindikatoren	64
expenditure of time	Zeitaufwand	84
group dynamic process	Gruppendynamischer Prozess	56
house of the Balanced Scorecard	Haus der Balanced Scorecard	53
key image	Leitbild	47
key indicator	Leitkennzahl	49
key objective	Leitziel	11, 48
learning process	Lernprozess	78
logo	Logo	48
Management Scorecard	Führungs-Scorecard	23, 72
milestones	Meilensteine	44
mission	Mission	40
moderation	Moderation	81
municipality	Kommunen	11
OAR-principle	ZAK-Prinzip	30, 54
objective	Ziel	10
Objective – Action – Ratio	Ziel - Aktion - Kennzahl	29
open structures	offene Strukturen	28

Glossary of keywords   English - German (b)

operational	operativ - nutzen	25
participants	Teilnehmer	80
perspective	Perspektive	11, 51
potentials	Potenziale	11, 25
process flow	Umsetzungsprozessl	22
project management	Projekt Management	71
project steps	Projektschritte	68
ratio	Kennzahl	30, 32
Reporting Scorecard	Berichts-Scorecard	23, 73
responsibility	Verantwortung	28
software assistance	Software Unterstützung	83
staff	Mitarbeiter	11
strategic	strategisch - entwickeln	25
strategic components	strategische Bausteine	44
strategic coordinate system	strategische Koordinaten	50
strategic horizon	strategischer Horizont	34
strategic project	strategisches Projekt	66
strategic questions	strategische Fragen	25
strategic ratios	strategische Kennzahlen	85
strategic reporting	strategische Berichterstattung	76
strategic topics	Strategische Themen	50
strategy map	Strategie-Landkarte	16
strategy workshop	Strategie-Workshop	78
strategy-focussed action	strategiefokussierte Aktion	54
success with BSC	Erfolg mit der BSC	87
target system	Zielsystem	50
uniqueness	Einzigartigkeit	23
values	Werte	37
vision	Vision	38

ABOUT THE AUTHORs

Dr. Herwig R. Friedag
born 1950, degree and PhD in economics
married, 2 adult children
Consultant at Friedag Consult, specialised in:
- Implementing Balanced Scorecard in companies
- Conducting workshops about
  Balanced Scorecard and innovation
- Voluntary commitment for 20 years head of the
  International Association of Controllers (IAC) PR-board
- Head of the IAC international work group

Hobbies: travelling, bike-tours, hiking, sports like
          volleyball and rowing (with oars!)

Address:
Dr. Herwig R. Friedag, Friedag Consult
Beskidenstr. 33, D 14129 Berlin
Phone: +49 30 80 40 40 00
Mail: consult @ friedag.com, Internet: www.friedag.com

Dr. Walter Schmidt
born 1950, degree in chemistry, PhD in economics
married, 2 adult children
Consultant at ask-schmidt: advanced strategy and
k(c)ommunication:
- Strategy development and -implementation
- Implementing Balanced Scorecard in companies
- Former member of the managing board of the
  IAC (International Association of Controllers)

Hobbies: writing, music, philosophy

Address:
ask Dr. Walter Schmidt, ask-schmidt
Schopenhauerstr. 93 k, D 14129 Berlin
Phone: +49 30 64 84 96 26
Cell: +49 172 318 40 11
Mail: walter @ ask-schmidt.de, Internet: www.ask-schmidt.de

Both authors operate the BSC-homepage www.scorecard.de

www.ingramcontent.com/pod-product-compliance
Lightning Source LLC
Chambersburg PA
CBHW030910180526
45163CB00004B/1778